II

THE WHITE WITCH OF WIMBLEDON: Memoirs of a Cockney Gypsy

THE WHITE WITCH OF WIMBLEDON: Memoirs of a Cockney Gypsy

BY E.M. SAVAGE-GREY

Library of Congress Control
Number-2011929128

e-mail: peggrey@comcast.net

CONTENT

This book is dedicated by Doreen
to her family, especially her children and
grandchildren, with hopes and dreams
for better lives for them because of her
everlasting love and devotion

ACKNOWLEDGEMENTS

Thanks and credit to the British Library in London for the support and cooperation of their staff in compiling gypsy research

Thanks and acknowledgment to:

Sarita F. Kainen for her continued encouragement and for giving me the air miles for London

Henrietta Jo Pace for her faith and for being a good listener

The British Polio Fellowship members who showed me what courage is

Personal thanks to Slim Flegg, the Mayor of Merton and Councillor, who allowed me to be Mayoress of Merton for a day and arranged for me to have a chauffeured ride to Westminster Abbey for the annual service and reception of the mayorality of London. It was an experience of a lifetime.

Last, but not least, all thanks, acknowledgment and credit to Doreen, my Cockney, Celtic friend, of Spanish

Rommany Gypsy heritage, a gifted psychic who endured a lifetime of abuse and physical handicap. Doreen was the inspiration for this book. She will charm you with her good heart and her courage. I am grateful for the opportunity to be her biographer and Yankee friend for two decades. I loved every minute of our literary journey.

PROLOGUE

Do not follow the path. Make your own path and leave a trail. Ralph Waldo Emerson

This is the story of a very special lady who overcame a life-long physical handicap, pain, abuse, and separation and neglect from her parents. She pulled herself up by her own bootstraps. She raised three children as a single mother. In this book, she shares her dreams, goals and faith in God and good people. Being a true Gypsy, Doreen never waivers in her love of family, children and animals.

She tells her story in bits and pieces. No drum roll. That's how her life plays out. This is Doreen's story of inspiration to everyone dealing with a physical handicap or abuse, neglect and a loveless life. Doreen reaches out and draws you into her world and her heart.

Doreen discusses her Celtic and Rommany Gypsy heritage. Gypsies have been given a bad rep in the twentieth and twenty-first centuries. The latest surveys guesstimate that there are one million Rommany Gypsies living in America. Your next door neighbor could be a gypsy. The Gypsies in Europe were targeted for extermination in the Holocaust. As many as one and a half million Gypsies were killed in the Holocaust during World War II. Their language, Rommany, was always passed down by word of mouth, and now its use is fading. Gypsy music, Flamenco music, lives on, along with Gypsy heroines of operas and books. And who doesn't want to have his or her palm read, and peek into the future?

Chapter 1

DOREEN GRINDLE-AN EVACUATION CHILD

As a child, Doreen's surname was Grindle. She said that she was five or six years old, when she first realized she had psychic tendencies, too young to understand. Now, looking back, she said that there were psychic incidents that she can remember but that she could not explain.

She said that she was about seven when she had a dream about a teacher going up the ladder toward a stain-glassed window. The teacher had a smock-like dress, mauve, with bits of purple pattern on it, and Doreen was watching her go up the ladder, higher and higher. Then the ladder fell back from the wall while she was on it.

The very next day, what Doreen had dreamed was happening in reality, and Doreen was running about screaming to whoever was around to stop the teacher from going up the ladder. No one would listen. She was very upset. Then, just as Doreen had dreamed, the ladder fell away from the wall and the teacher fell with it. Doreen never saw that teacher after that day.

She recalls, I was a loner as a child, and often wandered off in a world of my own. I never had imaginary friends as playmates, but as a child I had unexplained psychic incidents. Especially one incident when I was at the first evacuation home. Boulton House, Great Tew, Oxford. London was being bombed nightly by the Nazis. So children were evacuated by many buses from London to the countryside to the north of London. Hundreds of children were sent out of the city, in anticipation of a Nazi invasion; children of all ages, from little ones to teenagers. It was a lot of unhappiness, children wrenched from their parents. They didn't return home or see their parents for years.

I went to an institutional home, a school home for handicapped children. The institution was a long way from home, for a little girl who wasn't quite four years old in 1939. Mrs. Jessica Thomas was the governess of the first home. She mentions me in her book about the epic evacuation of hundreds of children by coach from London. Mrs. Thomas wrote about going around the London neighborhoods, a horn sounding at each house, taking children away from their parents and homes, in 1939.

In one neighborhood, there was a gathering of neighbors awaiting the coach and clearly ready for a scene. Mrs. Thomas went to assist the child, but the mother clung to her, Mrs. Thomas wrote. "Keep the child in London, if you want," said Mrs. Thomas. That child was Doreen. Mrs. Thomas wrote, Doreen was for coming along on the coach. That is how Doreen was removed from her home for more than six years.

The war clouds had gathered over Europe in 1939 and the flat-bottomed German boats were ready to land in England. The blitz, nightly bombing of London by the Nazis, was on. Doreen's aunts owned a teahouse in the East end of London, at the docks. When sugar came under rationing, they went out of business; but it was the blitz that leveled the property. A Coral Gables, Florida rabbi recalled reading about the famed British positive attitude and resilience: During the blitz, an elderly woman's flat was destroyed. A bobby found a bit of gin in a bottle under the debris and offered it to the woman. She rejected it and said, "Oh, no" that's for emergencies".

To this day, the Churchill War Room and Museum has copies of a poster in the gift shop with the slogan, "Be Calm and Carry On". It was to be used if the Nazis invaded England. The crown on the poster represented King George VI, about whom the Oscar-winning movie, "The King's Speech", was made. The poster campaign was never circulated since there was no Nazi invasion, and the poster was forgotten. Many decades later, it was discovered in a storeroom, and copied. It is a big seller in the War Room gift shop.

In those early years of World War II, the Brits mobilized to save their children by moving them out of London, including handicapped children like Doreen who moved in a peg-leg fashion with the caliper on her leg. Coaches of children were taken out of London to various evacuation centers in the countryside. Mrs. Thomas mentions in her book that one evacuation camp was bombed and children and teachers were killed.

In the early 1940's, the war news was not good. France had been invaded. England was next. The courage of the Brits was spurred on by Prime Minister Winston Churchill in a radio broadcast: "We shall fight in France, we shall fight on the seas and oceans, we shall fight with growing confidence and growing strength in the air, we shall defend our island, whatever the cost may be, we shall fight on the beaches, we shall fight on the landing grounds, we shall fight in the fields and in the streets, we shall fight in the hills; we shall never surrender".

WITH MARCY AT BOLTON HOUSE

Doreen was at her first evacuation home, Boulton House, a historic manor house in Oxford, when she made friends with Marcy Meadows, another evacuee. Marcy, if you are around and you read this, come forth because you were my witness to this incident that we both will never forgot. We talked about this event when we came back to London, after the War. You lived down Lieve Road, not far from Castletown where I lived, and we met again and greeted each other as old acquaintances do. At the end of the greeting, we talked about Boulton House, what we never forgot, both of us, and the fear that went with it.

We remembered the night that we were in our dormitory, eight children, but we were the only two who were awake. Marcy, you had pulled one of your teeth out, and I told you that a fairy would come and put money under your pillow, if you put your tooth there. There was some light in the room. What we saw that night stopped up both in our tracks.

It was the noise that came first, like a clump, clump, clump, coming through the door. We were shocked to see a black leg walking on its own, down the center of the room. It stopped at Marcy's bed, turned in, and leaned up against her bed. We froze and closed our eyes tightly, terrified to move or speak for what seemed like hours. There was no more noise from the leg, and we eventually fell asleep. We both awoke the next morning and talked about it.

It was a black leg, walking by itself – maybe a peg leg. With ghosts, you may only see the part that is the artificial part, probably an artificial leg. We heard the noise, the heavy clumping noise. It came through the door when we were talking. The door was on the left-hand side of the room and there was light, so you could see part of the bed. We were concentrating on the noise, and this object came into the room, and turned into the bed. It gave us such a fright. We were terrified, and shut up and went to sleep that night. Every time Marcy and I got together, we talked about that night.

READING ADULT BOOKS

At the same place, I remember walking into a room, I was very young, about five, and I was wandering about. I was on my own, very much a loner. At that time I couldn't read, only books like the one about the Engine, primary stage reading. There was a stack of books in the middle of the room, all piled up. As I walked toward the books, I saw that there was a red (adult) book on top of the pile of books.

There was a sunbeam coming through the window into the room, onto the red book. As I stood there, the book opened on its own. I picked it up and became aware that I could understand it, although I was still on first child's primary. I can't remember the name of the book. I jumped from primary to adult. The teacher did not know because I did not tell anyone. The books were probably novels. I could read the words. Thereafter, I could read the words in other books and understand them.

INTO THE WOODS AT BOULTON HOUSE

At the same place, Boulton House, I must have been five years old when there was an outing in the woods with the teachers to collect logs. I decided to follow my own path, away from the others. I was lost yet I had no fear. I felt at peace with nature, discovering toad stools and shrieking with delight at seeing door mice scuttling through the underbrush.

Dusk was falling quickly, but still I was making discoveries. I remember sitting on a large log, looking up at the moon and stars, with an incredible feeling of awareness of the universe, knowing, yet not knowing – some sort of force or power in me and around me. Having had my affair with nature, I picked up a couple of logs, tucked them under my arm and knew – despite being lost – my way back. Only to be met by a large gathering of strangers, my teacher and policemen.

I had been gone apparently two hours and a search party was in progress, going into different parts of the woods to look for me. Eventually, I met them. There I stood, wide-eyed; looking up into angry faces, with my logs still tucked under my arm, not understanding what all of the fuss was about.

A kindly large policeman spoke to me and chided me for causing so much concern. I was lead away, my hand firmly in the grasp of a teacher, logs still under my arm, but catching a glimpse of the moon again, so full and so large. I was fascinated with the full moon and kept looking upward despite the teacher's urging to look where I was going. I could not tear my gaze away from that moon.

QUEEN MAREY CHILDREN'S HOSPITAL

I went into Queen Mary Children's Hospital when I was a few months old and I was there for 18 months. I spent time in an iron lung, an enclosure that left me with a lifetime of fear of being enclosed and isolated. Nowadays, I cherish the windows in my bedroom, which is my solace, where I can look out onto the street with passers-by, pet-walkers and my sheltering oak tree that I named Arthur. My blackbird friends, Jack and Jill, stop by daily and perch on my fence. And I leave food for Wendy, the fox, who visits nightly for her dinner.

As an infant, I had an operation on my hip, but this operation did nothing at all to help the polio. The doctors called it an experiment. The first few years of my life were wasted on being on my back in a hospital as a baby. In later years, many other surgeries gave me some mobility. I was able to walk with my walking sticks, but now, in my 70's, I am wheelchair bound and living with post-polio syndrome.

I don't have too many memories of my father. He was rarely in my early life. His name was Walter Byron Grindle and he came from Blyth, Northumberland, blonde and blue-eyed, a true Norseman. He had met my beautiful Spanish, dark-haired, dark-skinned mother, named Miriam Christina Del Santo, in Hammersmith. I have dark skin, eyes and hair, almost black, like my mother and some of my cousins. I do feel a bit embarrassed about having Gypsy blood but, as one of my aunts told me, my grandfather's name was on my mother's birth certificate. I am a child of Rommany Gypsies from Spain. In all, my grandmother had 10 children, including my mother, with different fathers. There is certainly no pedigree in my blood. My father was a descendant of the Vikings with a surname of Grindle, or grinder, someone who ground swords or axes to perfection. My parents went through a form of marriage but Mum was not divorced from her first husband at that time and had a son by that marriage. So I became illegitimate.

I did not realize what that entirely meant until when I was at school and a school friend said to me, why have you in your name Grindle and your mother's name is different? I asked my mother about that and she eventually changed my name to hers.

My maternal grandfather was a Rommany Gypsy from Algeciras in Andalusia, Spain and early 1900's photos of my mother depict a beautiful Spanish Gypsy girl. Andalusia is in the southern part of Spain and is a historical nationality with a Moorish culture and history. Flamenco music and bullfighting originated in Andalusia. Thus, I had strong forces of heritage, the Viking and Celtic influence of my father and my mother's Spanish Rommany Gypsy genes from my grandfather, Jose Del Santo.

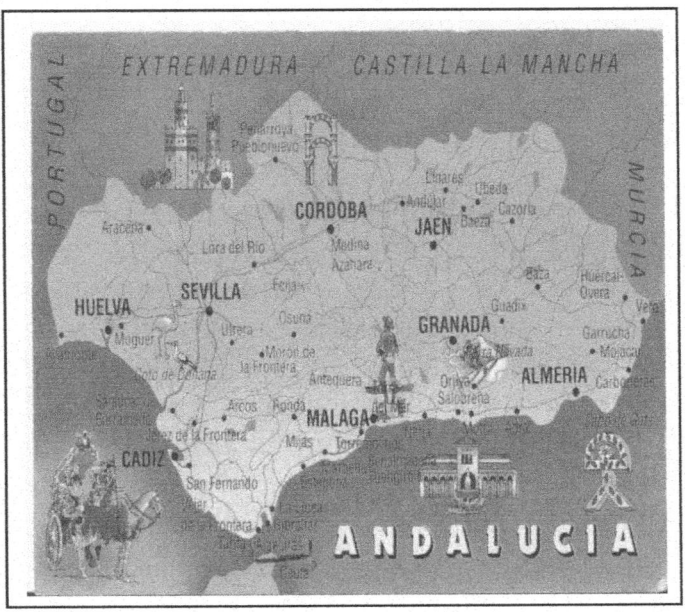

Algeciras in Andalucía is a port city, a jumping-off point to Morocco and the Canary Islands. Seville is the main city in Andalusia, which was conquered by the Moors (for 500 years) as well as the Romans, the Vandals and the Visigoths. The Spanish Inquisition, a tribunal under the supervision of the Spanish monarchy to uphold religious orthodoxy began in 1480 in Andalusia. Flamenco music was the combination of Gypsy, Arabic and Jewish cultures oppressed during the Inquisition. The director of the Museo de Baile Flamenco in Seville, Kurt Grotsch, credits the Inquisition for that unique bonding.

CHANGING KARMA

I became aware of Karma later in my life. Pattern begets pattern. A bad Karma can be passed on from generation to generation until you realize that you are following a bad Karma. I realized that this was happening to me, and I changed my Karma because I love my children more than myself, and my obligations were to my children. Now, their lives are patterning out better than mine. But despite my bad start in life, polio, hospitalizations, surgeries and pain, an absentee father, cruel separation from my Mum because of a horrific world war and, later, abuse from my mother and her disreputable boyfriends and then more abuse from the men in my life, I strove to change my bad childhood into a better life for me and my children.

I was born in 1935 on a Monday in a thunderstorm, in Mary Abbots Hospital in the Royal Borough of Kensington. After almost two years in the hospital with polio, I came home to Yeldham Road, Hammersmith, and No. 6 top flat. At that time, my parents were together. My father joined the army at the start of World War II. He never came back to me and my Mum.

EVACUATION - A CHILD'S NIGHTMARE

When I was only three weeks short of my fourth birthday, I went to live with strangers in Boulton House, Tew Park Greater Tew, Oxford. After that, I was moved to Fairlawn, Tunbridge Wells, Kent, then to Peckforton Castle, near Tarponley, Cheshire, from which I have bitter memories about my unhappy years there as a child.

My mother told me that I was a horror as a child -- defiant, strong-willed, despite being a victim of polio and having my right leg encased in a hideous caliper. I would fly up and down the street with a funny stiff-legged run, snatching other children's prams or balls and taking them off, much to the tears of my poor victims and their irate parents who did not know what to make of me. And my poor Mum would call me in, more often had to chase me up the street to get me, trying to console a very reluctant three-year-old whose freedom was threatened, with spit on the doorstep to rub it with my good leg. Even to this day I value my freedom of choice and will. And I am on my own today, although I love my kin and my close friends; I value my own privacy very much.

LIFE ON YELDHAM ROAD

I can remember clearly a sweet shop on the corner of Yeldham Road at that time. There was large News of the World ad sign above it, and I would be there to get a penny jumbo bag, with cards, sherbet and other sweets. And I remember going shopping with down King Street, Hammersmith, on my Dad's shoulders. Those kids on Yeldham Road must have been in their glory when I wasn't around.

I feel guilty and sad that I caused so much havoc down that street, but I did not remain on that street for long. War had started, and a coach came down the Yeldham Road, and several of the children, including me, were put into the coach. We were evacuees. I can remember the mothers, including mine, looking through the windows and waving and crying as we drove off in the coach, bewildered, to destinations unknown.

Boulton House was my first home. Although away from home and my Mum, and despite the ghostly black leg, Boulton House was happy for me. I remember sitting under a tree, shaded from the summer heat, having tea. Among the grown-ups, the War was always the main topic of conversation.

THE BABY AT BOULTON HOUSE

For me, I was happy to wander as far as they would let me, make imaginary cars or houses with corn shucks, play in the meadow, and watch the children from the nearby village dance round the maypole. I was the youngest, only four years old, the baby at Boulton House, and spoiled by the staff. Not everyone liked the evacuee children from London. On many occasions, when we went for walks through the village, we were verbally abused by the local children who called us names because we were different. I was to find out later that there would be more abuse from grownups because I was different.

Sunny days at Boulton House were carefree; Christmas was held with a large Christmas tree in the middle of the room, laden with colors of festivity, and presents of all sizes. On the right was a large log fire. I can always remember the music of Deanna Durbin, who sang "Waltzing High in the Clouds". Darker clouds were on the way. All good things must come to an end. For whatever reason, we were packed off to another place of evacuation, to Fairlawn Manor, Tunbridge Wells, Kent. This was not as carefree and happy as Boulton House, but it wasn't so bad, and I adapted to life there.

REMEMBERING FAIRLAWN TUNBRIDGE WELLS

I wasn't spoiled, like I was at Boulton House, however, there was a substitute: two goats, Billy was one, I can't remember the name of the other one. But I love animals and got to be great friends with them, until I was told off by one of the heads (owners) for paying too much attention to the goats.

I shall never forget when one of our girls nearly drowned at Fairlawn. We were all disabled kids, some had tuberculosis, some had polio, or kidney problems. Emmy Lou Zeller, had to wear something like a body splint.

We were in the Brownies, similar to the Boy Scout-Girl Scout program in America, and the leader took us on a ramble in the country. We had to cross a large pond by walking on large enough stepping stones in single file. As we were half-way across, one of the other girls had a fit and rushed poor old Emmy Lou into the water. I can see her now, going down, coming up, and the Brownie leader lying across the stepping stones and pulling her out.

With the heavy body splint pulling her down, Emmy Lou would have drowned if the leader had not been there to pull her out of the water. To make matters worse, her dark green woolen dress which was over her knees before she fell in now was down to her ankles. We all trailed home in silence with poor old Emmy Lou crying from her ordeal, soaking wet from head to toe, and clutching her very long frock away from her feet.

On a happier note, during our rambles here and there with the Brownie leader, we sometimes passed a mulberry tree fully-laden with big mauve mulberries. We stopped to pick them. They were a delicious fruit/berry, and I have never seen or tasted a mulberry since.

At Fairlawn, I was always getting a sore throat or some other illness. I always seemed to be in the sick bay. Sometimes they would forget all about me, and I would end up with no breakfast, no dinner or no tea. I seemed to have fewer illnesses after I had my tonsils removed.

However, we did not stay at Fairlawn. Soon we were packing our kit bags and gas masks and heading yet to another destination unknown.

Chapter 2

FOREBODING ABOUT PECKFORTON CASTLE

When we arrived at Peckforton Castle, near Tarponley, Cheshire, and I saw the castle for the first time, I felt uneasiness. Somehow I knew that I was not going to be as happy here as I was at Boulton House and not-so- bad Fairlawn. The Castle was huge, with a great big banquet hall, a minstrel gallery, archer's turrets, courtyards, a jousting green, a drawbridge and moat. It was built on a hill and at one point you could look down to see a panorama of miles length and breadth, with trains snaking their way to and fro.

We all arrived at Peckforton Castle late in the evening and sat down to a meal. From the time that I was sent away from London, before my fourth birthday, to Oxford, to Kent, and now to this place, I had never cried.

Now an overwhelming sadness and depression came over me and the tears fell. It was a whole new routine. Gone were the easy, carefree routine of Oxford, and the not bad routine of Kent.

THE LANCASHIRE HAG

Here we were met with a harsh, unloving Dickensian orphanage routine. The culprit is someone whom I called the Lancashire Hag. Ms. Jane Doe was a white, leather-skinned woman with steel gray hair done in what was the hairdo of that time, rolled all the way around her head. She had cold snake-like gray eyes to match her hair, no fullness of lips to give any indication of affection of any sort for the children, and a thin, cruel-down-slanted mouth to match her thin cruel heart.

One cannot have it all good always, and a little bit of discipline doesn't hurt anyone, however, we were all disabled children. We had been sent away from our loved ones and rarely saw our parents. It was at this place, the Castle, where I learned quickly about harsh reality. Ms. Doe had previously looked after boys. She made it quite clear that

Peckforton Castle was built between 1844-1850, as a Gothic manor house masquerading as a castle. Doreen was among the handicapped evacuee children who would live there during World War II. Peckforton Castle is located on the highest peak of Peckforton Hills in Cheshire. You may recognize Peckforton because the castle has been used as a setting for many movies and television shows.

she did not like girls. Bits of rags were pinned onto our chests with which to blow our noses. If one of us kids lost that bit of rag, whoever it was hard to answer to Ms. Doe with a clout round the head, no matter that some of us were thin and weak, or had a hump.

I began to feel sorrier for the weaker and smaller victims of the Hag than for myself. I would retrieve odd bits of lost rags and save some poor trembling kid from a clout by the Hag which would send any able-bodied kid spinning off their feet. So we stood no chance when the mood took her. She mostly made a bee-line for me. Although I was very afraid of her, I sort of developed an "I'll break you in the end, Hag" attitude toward her. I was only a child, crippled with polio.

HOW THE HANDICAPPED CHILDREN WERE ABUSED

The Hag taught me that, whatever I must do, I must try to walk without my caliper. This is how she taught me that lesson: I had done nothing, said nothing to her, but she would wait until I had my caliper off my leg, getting ready for bed, sitting on the edge of the bed, putting my nightdress over my head. She would stalk up behind me and whack me round the head so that I fell to the floor. I had no balance without my caliper on. From the time I returned to London, after staying at the Castle, to this very day, I have never worn another caliper.

One day, while attending church, I had a nose bleed and was sent back to the dorm with another girl. Who was there to meet me was the Hag herself, delighted at my plight. Probably the sight of blood excited her the more. She grabbed my hair and pushed me toward the basin. "Got a nose bleed, have you? We will soon get rid of that." She pushed my head down into the basin and nearly drowned me, with both taps funning full on. She ducked me again and again into the flow of water, which I cried and sputtered, trying to get my breath. Then she yanked me out, flung a towel round my face, and shoved me onto a bed.

She jeered to the other girl, and made the girl agree with her. I could not blame the girl as she was too afraid to stand up to the Hag. I got over that, but worse was to come. As you can imagine, life was very bleak and unhappy for us kids under the tyrannical treatment and strict Dickensian routine.

Mrs. Thomas, who was the headmistress, was not seen very often, only at special times. Ms. Jones, like the Hag, dealt with the children. I believe that she must have been there only part-time or possibly lived outside the Castle. At least she treated us kids better than the Hag. Of course, the Hag was one of the live-in staff, so she was constantly around. Never a kind word or action was shown by that hard-faced Lancashire woman during the years that we had to tolerate her cruelty, both mental and physical.

CHILDREN ARE TREATED CRUELLY

I will always remember one occasion which made me hate the Hag beyond all reasoning. One of my friends was Anita Toomey, a thin little girl whose disability was to do with her lungs or chest. Every morning we had to line up in our navy blue knickers and wait our turn for the sink.

God help us if we got out of turn or didn't follow up the girl in front, which so happened to poor Anita. For some reason, she didn't follow up quick enough for the Hag. So Ms. Doe pushed Anita so hard that the poor girl, instead of going toward the sink which if she had hit it would have been bad enough, fell against an iron cast bed with round, ball-shaped castors on it.

I can remember the thud her little chest made when she hit the iron frame. It left Anita gasping for breath as she sank to the floor, white faced, with her eyes closed. We all stood round frozen with horror and fear. How the Hag got away with that incident I will never know, because Anita was badly bruised for weeks. I vowed from that time on that I would somehow, someway, bring the Hag down. My time did come, later.

Whatever disability we kids had, she would ridicule and laugh and scorn us. If some poor kid had a deformed back with a hump, she would imitate the child's action. One little girl had rather large front teeth which protruded. The Hag would call her George Formby and gave her a whack around the head to go with it. That Hag certainly taught me some bitter lessons inside that institution. I was to learn more later on, on the outside.

USING THE HAIRBRUSH TO INFLICT PAIN

The difference of straight hair and curly hair made no difference to the Hag when she combed our hair, which was always with a steel comb. It made a difference to whoever had straight or curly hair. If your hair was curly, getting combed was a painful experience, and mine was curly.

The Hag relished it as she brought that comb from the forehead to the back of the head with no stopping for tangles or anything. I am sure that my head must have looked like a ploughed field after she finished with me. This went on day after day, year after year. You got off a bit more lightly if your hair was straight. I am quite surprised that I did not end up with straight hair for good. She must have known that we were gritting our teeth and holding back tears of pain. Whatever she did for us, whatever she had to do for us, was done with a spiteful or cruel action.

Peckforton Castle was in a rural area. That's why this abusive caretaker was able to get away with what she was doing to us. There were no authorities to check on what was happening in the Castle, home to hundreds of evacuee children. Further, the children did not see doctors regularly. During the War, the doctors were called up to the front.

LOOKING FOR SHIRLEY TEMPLE

There were good occasions, which were rare. The Yanks would come in convoys of lorries to visit the Castle, which had a lot of historic interest. They would come and put on shows for the kids and they brought goodies which we saw but hardly ever got.

Some of the luckier kids got Shirley Temple dolls, but I did not. As young as I was, I always seemed to be one step ahead, in my interest in and concern about treats. Eventually, this led to my getting into a lot of trouble.

PARCELS AND LETTERS FROM HOME INTERCEPTED

I did not have many visits from anyone, except my Mum, who rarely came to visit me. It was war-time and we were quite far away from London. I will always remember the occasional parcels from home. The parcels were given to us at morning prayer and assembly, so rare in fact that I could hardly keep my excitement under control. We were not allowed to open the parcels or letters. Letters were read to us by the staff and any letters written by us were also read by staff.

One day I received a parcel from home and all the longings of the unattainable was too much for me. I began to make a hole with my finger through the brown wrapping. Bit by bit, my finger burrowed deeper until I came across something hard. Still too excited to stop, I made a hole that was getting bigger and bigger until I could just about see two candy fish, pink and yellow. So I had a scratch and a lick. That's about all I had, because the parcel was taken away from me and I never saw those fish or whatever else was in the package again.

WHAT HAPPENED TO THE SWEETS?

I began to think about seeing lots of sweets that the Yanks brought. What happened to those sweets? We didn't have any. Then, there was my one rare parcel from home with the two candy fish. I didn't have them. So where were all of these sweets?

For the occasion candy we kids had received, it did not add up. We were given three or four sweets occasionally. It was all we got. It was so bad that I had a little tin that I used to put my rare sweets in. Perhaps I'd have a look or a few licks to make them last.

I used to daydream that, when I grew up, I would have one room filled to the ceiling with sweets and chocolate. That dream never came true, but I made up for all the sweets that I didn't have later by working in Fuller's chocolate factory. After a few weeks there I couldn't look at the sweets without feeling 'Yuk'. The love of sweets led to my downfall at the Castle.

THE NAUGHTY NIGHTTIME CAPER

For some reason, I was moved into the next dormitory and my bed was facing a tuck cupboard. I saw the dreaded Hag go to the cupboard before lights were off. She appeared to be taking items from the cupboard and putting them in a bag. The night of discovery came when she left the key in the cupboard and I no longer was able to contain my curiosity.

Making sure plenty of time had passed, I crept out of bed in the dark and hopped over to the cupboard. A couple of the kids in my room heard me and I let them in on what I was doing. I turned the key and opened the cupboard. I put my hand in the cupboard and felt items of different shapes and sizes of things. I pulled out a rather large shape. It was the biggest bar of chocolate that I had ever seen in my very young life.

I could not believe it. My hand began to tremble with excitement as I discovered other goodies: bars, toffee, and sweets of all kind. It was like Aladdin's Cave, but it was not precious gems that I was discovering. It was sweets. By this time, I lost control and was handing out chocolate and sweets to all of the kids in my dorm. 'Now listen, Kids', I said, 'when you have finished with your wrappers put them in your gasmask case and empty it when we go out to the air raid drill'.   We had occasional air drills. This, they all agreed to do.

THE NEXT DORM JOINS THE SWEETS PARTY

The next door dorm heard all the noise and the kids were coming in, wondering what was going on. What a lovely noise of rustling paper! More chocolates and sweets were handed out and the kids in the next dorm also were told to put their wrappers in their gas mask cases.

My naughty discovery was soon to be discovered. But at least I realized where all the sweets and chocolate that was meant for us kids was going – maybe to the Black Market. The sweets were probably leaving the Castle in the Hag's bag. No wonder all we got were a miserable few sweets now and then. Anyway, she never got that night's supply.

We all had a good old feast. But it was a bar of toffee which brought about my downfall. Poor old Cathy Martin in the next bed to me had a weak bladder and had to get up at 10 o'clock at night to go to the loo. The Hag would come back up to the dorms with her torch a-flashing and get Cathy up for a wee. As the Hag arranged Cathy's pillow, whoops, there lay the bar of toffee that I had given Cathy during the sweets and chocolate raid. Cathy had not put it away.

Oh, my, questions, questions. Cathy had a few weeps and this would have gone on except that my name was mentioned. I had no choice but to own up, whereupon I was dragged out of bed, by my hair as usual, and made to stand in the corner of the room. With my caliper off, it was very difficult for me to stand. It must have been for more than an hour. I stood there alone and cold, but at least very full up.

THE TRIAL AND A FRIEND WHO SUPPORTED HER

The next morning at assembly I was put on trial for my naughty confectionary party. Mrs. Thomas was there. All of the teachers and children, whether or not they were aware of it on the previous night, now knew what I had done. But at least most of them had more sweets and chocolate in one night than they had received in the years we had to have the unfortunate fate to be where we were.

One little voice piped up from all the girls, Mandy Hill, bless her. "Never mind, Dor," she said. At least one voice stood up for me and we were always friends, at the Castle and when we returned to London, where we both attended Queensmill Road School.

I remember Mandy when we were performing in an opera, "Maritana", at Queensmill. We were rehearsing our parts, and poor Mandy played the part of a member of a Gypsy tribe. She had unusually long legs, but owing to her disability, she walked with a bent knee gait. There were about 25 to 30 pupils who made up the whole of the Gypsy mob, and they had to go backwards and forwards with hands joined together and sort of skip.

On instructions from the drama teacher, "Right girls forward" and "Now girls backward", Mandy and her long legs skipped a couple of steps backwards and fell down the back of the stage platform completely out of view of all of us. Thank heaven, she was not hurt; little wonder, the dreadful noise she made to go with it. Gradually, a rather bedraggled, but lovable Mandy, clambered back onto the stage, her hat askew.

I always felt a sense of sadness with that girl. The last time I ever saw Mandy was quite a few years after leaving school when I was 16. I was coming over Westminster bridge and I saw her but she didn't see me. I can't remember whose car I was in but I remember looking out of the back window until she was out of sight.

THE LANCASHIRE HAG ENDANGERS DOREEN

The last days of the Lancashire Hag began one day when we were lined up for a bath. When it was my turn, she put the boiling hot tap on, filled the tub, but did not run the cold tap. I stepped into the bath, and before I could get out, she pushed me down into the boiling half-filled bath. I just screamed and got out of that bath quicker than I got in, but she had pushed me down hard enough to scald my legs and backside. I stood and held to the side of the bathtub and screamed and screamed with pain.

I must have made one helluva noise because in rushed Mrs. Thomas, the head mistress, who we did not see too often. By the time Mrs. Thomas arrived in the bathroom, the crafty Hag had turned on the cold tap, but my burned backside and legs were sufficient evidence for Ms. Thomas to know that I was not screaming for nothing. The result is that, from that day to this, I cannot get into a very hot bath – it has to be lukewarm for me.

WRITING TO MY MUM

An opportunity arose a few weeks after this, when we were writing letters. As I previously noted, letters were always intercepted, incoming and outgoing. Miss Canton was in charge of our group and while her mind was on another matter, she told me to seal my envelope myself, whereupon I seized the opportunity to scribble on the inside of the envelope flap, "Please Mum, take me home, we are being cruelly treated". Thank heaven that the message got home to my mother. There must have been more complaints from other parents about that cruel woman who put fear and misery into our lives during the time we were at Peckforton Castle.

Peace was to reign at last. A few months after that incident in the bathtub, the Hag walked into our dorm in a black coat, so unusual from the white uniform she always wore. Her last statement was directed to me – "I suppose you are satisfied, Grindle". She turned and walked out of the room, never to be seen again at Peckforton Castle. I was smiling; I was satisfied. In her book, "Help for the Handicapped", Mrs. Thomas never wrote one word about the abuse inflicted on us by the Lancashire Hag.

I did not allow these awful events to affect me – rather I learned from them. The cruel woman helped to toughen me up for future setbacks that were awaiting me in the years to come.

She taught me, also, that I would be vulnerable and helpless as long as I relied on my splint, so I was determined to get rid of it when I came home.

END OF THE WAR AND GOING HOME

I was 10 years old when I returned to London. I had been away from home for more than six years. I thought that coming home would be utopia. I had daydreams of fantasy that I would belong to my family, no more cruel people to make my life a misery anymore, and I would have all the sweets and chocolates that I could eat. However, reality is another thing. I reveled in the happiness of being told that we were going home, the end of the war, red, white and blue ribbons in our hair, the bells ringing, piling into a coach to go back to London. And then, home.

Home was a basement with a gate and 13 steps which led down to the front door, bars at the windows, Castletown Road, West Kensington, in an old four-story building. Apparently the basement was for the servants' quarters, like

Upstairs Downstairs. It was dark and depressing from the front door through the entire flat. You walked into a tiny kitchen and scullery. Next to that was a coal cellar. It was damp and large slugs used to leave their silver trail wherever they went. A small step led to the large front room. The war was over, but there was no instant prosperity in England. Rationing lasted well into the 1950's and frugality forever bound my life. To this day, in the 21st century, scrimping, saving and shopping at boot sales and thrift shops is my way of life.

I remember, in that basement flat, that Mother had a chiming clock which chimed whatever hour the day was. I thought it was a rather pleasant sound whenever it chimed from the inside of the front room. Looking through the barred windows, you could see people's legs walk by and occasionally a dog would cock its leg and we would get a cascade of wee wee down the stairs.

My mother could not accept me. I returned to her after years of hospitalization and homes for the handicapped. I didn't understand it then, but I understand it now. She had one boyfriend after another. They used to drink together. She was an abortionist, in and out of jail. I was in the way. Home life was one fight after another, mostly about money. I always stuck up for my mother. It cost me more than once. On one memorable occasion, I had the hiding of my life. I must have been 15.

My mother was fed up with me. She had never raised me. She had been free of me for almost 10 years and could do what she wanted. Then I came back into her life. She felt that I was making demands on her. You could not blame her. She had been through the war. She did not have such a great life, born and brought up in a roadhouse and hit with a great big stick on occasion.

It took a lifetime for me to understand and come to terms with those early years. I later determined that I would never put my children through the neglect and abuse that I had endured.

Chapter 3

AN OPEN LETTER TO MY DAD

Dear Dad,
I can remember you when I was a child. Fair wavy hair and very blue eyes. Your Adam's apple was very prominent. You used to take me on your shoulder down King Street, Hammersmith. I remember having a red top, but I could not spin it. You used to do it for me. I remember putting tiny sweets up my nose once and I almost choked. You held me upside down until they all came out.

I remember No. 6, Yeldham Road, Hammersmith when you and Mum lived in the top flat with a German helmet in the bedroom. I caught polio and went to the hospital. I was put in an iron lung. You came to see me in the hospital once and brought me a chocolate Easter egg. You never came again. Then, at the start of the Second World War, I was taken away as an evacuee child. You went into the Army and never returned to us. I was sent to three evacuation homes in six years and you never wrote to me or came to see me.

42

I saw you once more at the end of the war. Then you were gone. You rejected me, Dad, just like I was later rejected by Mother. You broke up with Mother, and you met another lady. You had another daughter. You could have been in touch with me to make sure that your younger daughter and I would get to know each other. You denied me that, just as you denied staying in my life and being my father.

Every time I eat chocolate, I think of you. When I watch films of the Second World War, with soldiers marching with their chin helmets, I think of you. And I wonder why you rejected me. After the War, my life was a nightmare with my Mother being drunk most of the time, so many men coming and going, not being at home often. After I came home from school as a teenager in London, there was no nice dinner waiting for me. Often, I went hungry.

School was my only haven, considering my dreadful home life. I passed several Chamber of Commerce exams which could have taken me forward to have a good career. But there was no one around to give me any encouragement. Mostly, I had to put up with my Mother's bad moods. I could never do anything right, as far as she was concerned. She bought her boyfriends new suits and, for one, a new car. But for me, her only daughter, there was only indifference. That treatment only made me strong and able to accept whatever came my way. No self pity.

I wanted children, whether I was married or not, and I had three children. It was hard being a single mother, having to work, but I did my best. And now I have my own family to love, lovely children and grandchildren. If I had support, I would have loved to become a midwife, a jet pilot, a member of the police force, a magistrate or an auctioneer. My love of children would have led me to become a children's doctor. My love of animals would have made me a veterinarian or an employee at a zoo. One of those dreams could have been a reality, if only I had a chance, or some encouragement when I was younger, instead of indifference and rejection. Sometimes, you can bend over backwards to help family and friends and get no appreciation, no cuddle of thanks or a phone call just to say Hello. Shut up, Doreen! You're getting maudlin.

Chapter 4

USING YOUR THIRD EYE TO BE PSYCHIC

You know you're psychic when you're psychic. I realized that I was somehow different at an early age. There is something called a psychic line. You see that line in my hand? It's on both hands. It goes round from the little finger all the way down. Look through the magnifying glass. Now look at that line. It's more pronounced on the right hand.

Some people don't know they're psychic, some people pretend that they are, but they're not. Everybody can be psychic, to a small extent. If you are calling someone on the telephone, and they are calling you at the same time, that could be a telepathic experience. It all ties in with being psychic. The scientific evidence for parapsychology or telepathy is mixed. Those who practice Eastern religions, where meditation is de rigueur, claim they have telepathic experiences during meditation.

Researchers report that even Albert Einstein did not dismiss the possibility of telepathy.

You're using your "third eye" in readings. The third eye, inner eye, is a mystical and esoteric concept referring in part to the ajna (brow) chapra in certain Eastern and Western spiritual traditions. In Indian and East Asian iconography, you will see a dot, eye or mark on the forehead of deities or enlightened beings, such as Shiva, the Buddha or any number of yogis, sages and bodhisattvas. The third eye is often associated with visions, clairvoyance (ability to observe chakras and auras), precognition and out-of-body experiences. People who have allegedly developed the capacity to utilize their third eye are sometimes known as seers.

When I do a reading, I get information about the people who are my clients, like family matters, all sorts of things, similar to listening to a radio. When I do the tarot cards, I'm setting myself up for reception. It's like trying to get reception on a radio, you don't want interference. You're building yourself up for reception. If I don't sleep before I see people, I can't do a reading. It has to be clear. You wear yourself out reading the tarot cards.

I have to concentrate on the person for whom I am doing the reading. I have to be good, because many of them will come back again. That proves that something is happening. It's not bragging. They are from all walks of life: different countries and various professions, ages and marital status. I go to a party, with eight, but I can't do all eight readings. I don't have enough time. People have heard of me, but I don't know who they are. Spanish people, French. Readings are half an hour. Sometimes I am oblivious of time and I go on and on.

Karma is trying to project to people. It's trying to straighten them out by helping them realize their karma or life's path. For me, it was not being bitter toward my mother, it was showing her all the love I could. You have to take on all the problems of another person. You have to make sure the karma doesn't go into your own path.

I stopped the bad karma in my family, with great difficulty. It's a pattern. Karma can go from one generation to another, like my grandmother, born in a workhouse, very poor. Workhouses go back to the 1800's, There was no social security or public housing and assistance for poor families. My mother was born in 1903 in a workhouse. My family's karma goes back three or more generations.

If you don't realize what your karma is, you will follow the same pattern as your grandmother – illegitimate children, you know what I mean, one man after another, promiscuous. You have no luck from your father, no luck from your mother. You're like a ship without a sail. You don't know where you belong.

PERSONAL LIFE WAS ASKEW

My personal life was still askew in my 20's and 30's. It took me a long time to become aware of the karma, the pattern. I turned my life around because I loved my kids. I thought that I had to stop my family karma; if I did, my kids would have better lives. Look at the photos of my children and grandchildren. They have become what I wanted to project, not self pity. If you don't change your karma, it goes into the next generation. If you love your family, you sacrifice. I am laid back. No taking from others, only giving.

You need to have honesty. My mother had no money. I was out of work, in my 20's. I had my oldest daughter, Nan . . . Nancy. She was in a home for children at the time. I said that I did not want that for Nan or my younger two children any longer. I had to steal for food. To go in a shop and shoplift was something that filled me with repulsion. But when you are hungry, and you have a flat in a basement, you do things to survive.

My mother didn't want to know me, she was living with another man, and I was too much of a nuisance to her. Eventually I worked for some builders, menial jobs. I worked in factories. I have high certificates of education. I ended up in a chocolate factory. I ate chocolate on the job until I was sick of it. I worked in an office, at the Chamber of Commerce, as a journalist. After World War II, there was peace in England but no jobs. Through it all, my girlhood in school and my early jobs, my mother never encouraged me. She wouldn't pay for me to go for further schooling, but she could buy a car or other presents for her boyfriends. You tell me if that isn't unfair and misery.

It was always, "get out of my way". She took all the confidence from me. I had no confidence to go in an office and seek a higher level job. . . yet I had the ability and intelligence to excel in public school when I was growing up and to pass exams in half the time required to complete them.

I worried about Nan, my oldest, whom I had placed in a children's home. I was in the quicksand, I was sinking. It went through my head, prostitution, but I didn't do it. I had that much respect, self-respect,

I wouldn't go that low.   But I took to "nicking" stuff in stores.

DOREEN AND MARGIE "NICK" FOOD

Margie would keep a watch out when we went to stores, and I would go in. I would nick sandwiches and cheese and things like that. I told her to keep the store clerk talking, and I stole food. One time, she went out of the shop and left me in there when she heard the sausages rattling. I had put them in a bag. When confronted by the store clerk, I said that I had been shopping somewhere else, and that's why I had sausages in the bag.

I asked for something else, and he said they didn't have it, and I said I will try another shop. So I got away with sausages and cheese and milk. What I did, it makes me feel ill. You lower your self esteem. That's why I understand people. Margie accidentally broke my toes once; she had a scooter and caught my toes and put me out of work.

Margie – At the time that we got together, she was meeting blokes and going to many parties. I met her in a pub, and we became close friends. She was quite pretty. She moved into the basement flat with me for awhile to share costs. It was very cheap at that time. Low rent.

CLIENTS COME FROM DIFFERENT COUNTRIES

It took years, but I started to build a clientele who came to see me for psychic readings. To this day, they come to see me. Clients come from different countries, such as Spain, France, Scotland, Hawaii, America and from all over England. Sometimes I travel to France or Spain as the guest of some friends who seek readings. It doesn't matter who they are or where they come from. All of them don't have problems. Some come to see me because they are curious, some just come for a reading. Some want to know where they are going, want direction, and want you to help them on their way.

Some seek guidance in their career or can't decide what career to go into. You see blockages in their lives, a problem to overcome. You tell them that they are in a blockage situation, and not to make too many decisions at once.

I have been doing this for most of my life. It comes natural. But I also read tarot cards, what you call a quadrant, four cards.

And these four cards hold messages. You just look at the cards, and you know how to read them. The client picks the cards. And everyone's cards are different. The cards that they select themselves tell me what's going on.

The clients don't tell me about their lives, I tell them. Different cards mean different things. In combination with another card, the cards take on a new meaning. For instance, a card with the death symbol does not mean death of the person. It may signify the end of something, a job or relationship, and mark a new direction for you. Readings are tiring because they take a great deal of concentration. It is rewarding to me that someone can get some help from my reading. I tell people about options, and encourage them to use their potential.

Women are more into their feelings, concerned about romantic and work relationships, not so much the future. Some of them want to know what lies ahead of them . . . don't we all? You have to be gentle with them, you must not go into anything horrible to upset them. People go through bad times but they want a better future. If I see the death of a person in their future – that of the client or a loved one – I do not forecast it. I will advise them to contact or go to their loved one(s).

Have I done this? Yes. Have I been correct. Sadly, yes.

People want reinforcement. They want to hear something positive and they want direction. People are affected by their environment. However, just because someone has had a bad past doesn't mean that person will have a bad future. As to whether they have family, or someone close to encourage them, just look at me as an example. I turned my life around for myself and my children. Bad experiences can be turned around and you can have good experiences. There are certain people in this world who can do that, but not all. There is no vanity with me, no ego. I may give a better reading with one person as opposed to another. I can't be that bad a psychic if they come back time and time again.

I don't charge too much money. It's not about money. Some psychics are charging a dreadful amount. I don't think it's worth that. Psychics aren't necessarily fortunetellers, they're people with life experiences. I think that life – what you've gone through in life – makes you more aware, more sensitive to the feelings and psyches of others.

Having polio and not being able to walk most of my life has made me more aware of and sensitive to the problems of people. I have time to reflect, and this gives me more insight into the problems of others. I had numerous surgeries all of my life, but my poliomyelitis has continued to progress. I would say that prescience is a sense, like blind people have when they can't see others but have a great sense of awareness of their surroundings and of people. I don't really need the "carrot cards", as tarot cards are jokingly called. Not every day.

THE GINGER CAT

Dreams can be the precursor of the reality. I had a dream one night, and told my friend and co-worker, Shirley, that I dreamt of a ginger cat and it wasn't moving, it was just looking at me. I thought it may mean that I was going to have a ginger cat. Stray cats have found me. I love all animals.

This is what happened regarding the ginger cat: at work, Mary was talking about cats, and I asked if she was talking about a ginger cat, and she said no. Then I went to my desk and I found a box on my table. Inside was a ginger cat teapot from a friend. It clearly wasn't a real cat. The ginger cat was stoically looking at me. . .

the ginger cat that I dreamt about, Shirley came in and screamed, "The Ginger Cat". Dreams have meaning.

THE WHITE WITCH OF WIMBLEDON

Some years back, I didn't have a cat. I lived in South Wimbledon in the four-story flats, on the ground floor. I always loved animals and I would take in strays. If there was a stray dog running around, I would corral the stray to take it off the street and feed it. Once I took a dog to the police station, and it became a police dog. I found out after.

It was the same situation with Witch. I didn't have a cat at the time, but I had a very fat jolly friend who lived on the next floor up. She used to come down and have a cup of tea with me, and every Saturday we would go out and buy up Sutton. Lisa lived upstairs and came down in the morning and the afternoon. One day I told her that my Hoover was broken and I wanted to get a broom. I was very poor at that time. She told me there was a wholesaler in Sutton closing down, so we went there.

The store was going out of business and almost everything had been sold. I went into the shop and I said to the man behind the counter, 'Excuse me, I know you're closing down, but do you happen to have an old broom, any old broom?' He said, "Yes, Madam", went to the back of the store and came out with a witch's broom. He said, "That's all I can do for you. You can have this broom for one pound 50". I said, "That will do, so I can sweep up".

So off we went home with the broom. We were sitting in arm chairs and I was having a cup of coffee, and I had left the broom up against the door. I told Lisa, laughingly, with my psychic readings and now the broom, they will call me the White Witch of Wimbledon. I told her all that I needed was a black cat. I couldn't have that broom without a black cat. We were laughing about that. This is gospel truth. Ask Lisa.

She told me that she had to go upstairs to make her old man's dinner. I told her that I would see her later. I used to leave the door open for the kids to come in straight from school. They would come dashing in the door to go to the toilet or what. That day, a black cat walked in my door, walked down the hallway. That's strange. The cat walked into the kitchen, jumped on the cooker, never left. Stayed.

I said, that's Lisa, playing tricks on me. She's borrowed a black cat from somebody and pushed it in the door. I honestly thought that.

I always feed animals, so I gave the black cat some milk and food. There it stayed and decided not to go out anymore. I said to Lisa, do you know anything about the black cat we were talking about? Do you remember earlier on we were talking about a black cat to go with my broom? Just go into my kitchen and have a look. She said, Doreen, where did it come from? I said I was going to ask you that. She said, "I swear on my life, Doreen, I don't know where it came from". I said, 'I swear, Lisa, I don't know, it just walked in my door.' We kept the cat, beautiful big, black cat. There's a photo. It looked like an Egyptian cat. I called her Witch.

At first, Witch would not let me touch her, and she wouldn't let me cuddle her, because I like to cuddle cats and dogs. She kept her distance but she respected me. It was a gradual bonding. It took actually a year for me to be able to touch her.

One day, I was going on about her fur, she had this crescent on her head, like a half moon upside down. I was pushing the fur back, and she had a circle on the chest, and when I opened it, I couldn't believe my eyes, it was the shape of a star, the shape of my pentacle. I couldn't believe it. I thought, maybe I made it to look like that, but I pinpointed it in the middle and it came out again when I moved the fur on her head. Witch had a pentacle!

That summer, when I moved from that flat, the Witch moved with me. And then one day, Witch died at my feet. But I had her a long time.

ANNE AND HER FAMOUS SON

One of my clients, I will call her Anne, comes usually every year, a very nice lady, a nurse. I met her while doing readings at a hospital. I do charities for schools and hospitals, fund raising at Nelson Hospital, dressed up in my Rommany Gypsy gear, gold earrings and tasseled shawl. We were charging a pound for a five-minute reading. A little school girl was taking the pounds as they came to see me.

In walked this lovely, attractive lady, elderly but attractive, and she sat down in front of me for a reading. I told her that there were certain situations in her life, and I told her some truths about what was going to take place, and that she had a very famous son, and that he was going to sign a contract and was going to go to the top. This happened. I learned later that her son played James Bond in the movies.

She was so astounded about what I said; she said that she wanted to meet with me again. She came to see me, and had a longer reading and more information came out of that reading. We became fast friends. She didn't live far from me. We had a bottle of wine between us occasionally in the evening, American wine. She would get a bit tickly.

One day, I went to finish off the bottle. We can't waste that. I said let's finish this bottle, Anne, and she was not sitting very far from me. I got up to do something and Anne was standing up, about to put something on the side. When I got up, I fell over and pushed her by mistake as I fell down, and she fell over the bed, and what was so funny, she had the drink in her hand and never spilled a drop. I was laughing so much, I said 'Look at your drink'. She said, "Well, I'm Irish and Irish people don't waste their drink". We both laughed. I never forgot that for a long time.

THE *"MARIE CLAIRE" MAGAZINE STORY*

Anyone who comes to see Doreen usually has heard about her by word-of-mouth. She also has received recognition in a British publication. Doreen was included in a story entitled "Predictions" in the November 1992 issue of "Marie Claire", UK Edition, published in London. "Marie Claire" had just received the Magazine of the Year Award from "Media Week" and won the Amnesty International Press Award for 1992 in the periodicals category. Marie Claire emphasized that Doreen "gave advice, detailing options that are available but stressing that you have to make decisions".

Chapter 5

MADAME DOREENA
Reader of the Tarot and Palm

When Doreen Ingram and this author met in September, 1992, I did not know that we would share a literary voyage for almost two decades. On the other hand, she must have known immediately. She questioned me about my newspaper background and talked about her goal of writing a book. She told Sheila and me about the happenstance of realizing that she was a psychic, something that she had never planned, and told us stories about some of the people who had consulted her.

Doreen started reading tea leaves for friends at work, for fun, during breaks for tea. She worked at a print shop for which the team did sorting and mailing. Reading tea leaves has been called tasseography, a form of psychic reading that depends on the psychic's ability to interpret the formation of the residue in one's tea cup. Reading tea leaves is not done traditionally by Gypsies, who are more likely to do fortunetelling and reading Tarot cards. Reading tea leaves in England is significantly done by village fortune tellers.

Doreen discovered early on that she had great accuracy in interpreting the residue of tea leaves in tea cups. What started out as fun, to while away time and amuse her co-workers during tea breaks, became part of her life. And, so Madame Doreena found her calling.

To this day, she reads tea leaves. Ironically, in 2005, Doreen served traditional English breakfast tea to a houseguest. One morning, after the ritual breakfast tea and chat, she looked into her tea cup and frowned. 'Oh, dear', she said, 'this is not good'. Remnants of the tea leaves had settled into the distinctive shape of the map of England, and there were three separate particles of tea leaves within the outline. 'Three bombs', she predicted. A few weeks later, the city of London suffered explosive devices. Three bombs in the transportation system.

In more recent years, as the progression of poliomyelitis has become post polio syndrome, Madame Doreena is bedridden. For an occasional client, she holds court in her bedroom, complete with her little black stray/foundling cat, Minnie, curled up on the corner of the bed. Guests sit on the edge of her bed. Her enthusiasm and credibility is never questioned by those who come to see her.

ARE THERE ANGELS?

Doreen believes in the protection of angels or some spirit or spiritual person who looks after us. She had a few strong experiences that go beyond coincidences. There was one such incident one summer night when the window was left open in her front room. She explained:

It was four in the morning when a bag doll which hung near her bed fell down and knocked some things on the floor, which woke me up. About half an hour later, I was dozing off when I noticed a torch going up and down my hallway. I then became wide awake and watchful. I saw a tall figure in the hallway going back and forth to the front room. I always left my door keys on the inside of the front door although it was always locked. The moving torch made me realize that she had a burglar walking about.

I was not afraid. I resented him going about my home. I think he was aware that someone was in the flat, as he stood in the darkness by my bedroom door and was moving into the doorway. So I thought that I must do something immediately. I started to growl, like a dog. Grrrrrrrrr. And he fled out the front door. He had cut himself somehow, and left some blood on the door handle. I called the police. They had a forensics expert check for the blood. The police officer laughed when I explained how I banished the burglar. Later, I looked to see why the doll bag fell. The hook that it was hanging on had not broken. And the doll bag rope had not snapped, either. I was warned. A half-hour before the intruder was in my flat, the bag fell. I don't believe that it was a coincidence. My angel or guide had warned me on that occasion and on other occasions as well.

PREMONITIONS

Madame Doreena gets premonitions any time of the day. She tries to be detached so that when she sees the client, she concentrates on that person. To some extent, she uses extra sensory perception. She charges herself up before meeting people for a reading. She must relax to get her heartbeat down. She said that you need to be relaxed or you won't have good perception.

Doreen said that people want to know where they're going. You concentrate on that, tell them what their options are, and that they're going to be okay at some point. Sometimes there are situations they have to face, and they may not be alright at that time, but they are going to come out of it alright. She finds clients' future in-between their past and their present. Author William Faulkner said it better: "The past is not over, it's not even past".

How does she know the things that are coming up in the future? She reads the Tarot cards. Cards are the receptors. People who visit with her lay the cards for themselves. She doesn't touch any cards. Sometimes a negative card will show up, usually the negative card shows up in the past. It relates to stormy situations in the past.

The black card is the worst card you can get, evil. She believes that there is nothing good about that card whatsoever. But next to a good card, it means you are coming out of a recession, a bad situation. No two cards are alike. Each one of those cards is a symbol of your life, your health. She has seen life-threatening situations and has warned a few clients when she determined that their lives were in danger.

When she first starts a layout of cards with a client, she explains that there are two things that she will not tell: when he or she is going to die or when he or she is going to face a tragic situation. She will not tell someone something that she feels is horrible, like they have a child that's going to die. She says that "if I can forewarn them about a situation, that they can change, I will tell them. The things that cannot be changed, I will not tell them".

SHE GAVE A WARNING

A young woman came to see her once, and she told the young woman not to go home that evening. Doreen felt very bad vibes about the young woman going back to her home. Doreen told her that her partner was a psychopath.

'I was very concerned about her,' said Doreen, 'and even offered to let her stay at my flat. The client went to her sister's home. A couple of days later, she went back to the flat for her belongings, and it was like a bomb had hit. Her boyfriend had gone berserk and destroyed everything in the flat that the couple shared.'

The clients rely on you, so you don't manipulate their lives; that's very unfair.

A SENSE OF FAIR PLAY

She said 'From my childhood, I had a furious temper. But I also had a sense of fair play. I realize today that that could have been because of the regimentation I experienced in the homes for handicapped children as an evacuee child. I suppressed my feelings because of fear of punishment, but I never let go of my outrage at injustice for myself and the other handicapped children. Time and time again I attacked people who wanted to pull me apart, even friends who I discovered were not my friends.

The friends that I have over the years are my gems, to the end of their lives. I did like school, after coming back from the WWII evacuation because my whole life, at that time, was dreadful. I had a dream of being reunited with my Mum, being at home, and the end of fear and strict routine. It was not to be.

I came away from early childhood memories of being an evacuee child only to find that my Mum, the very person on whom I had pinned my hopes and who at least would show me some love and a sense of belonging, rejected me. I have read that the truth is, eventually everyone in your life is going to hurt you. You just have to decide who is worth the pain.'

BAD KARMA BEGETS BAD KARMA

She explained, 'It is only now that I have accepted my Mum's rejection without anger and hate. As I have learned over the years, bad karma begets bad karma. Pattern follows pattern, until either self-realization or someone higher in our universe directs your course. I now realize that all of that bad karma that I had, I had to go through, to give me the wisdom and compassion that I have and not self-pity and bitterness.

I can honestly say that at this very time of my life I feel none of those destructive emotions to want to get back at people who have hurt me or society that has let me down. I believe in the law of averages, what we do bad to others or to ourselves is paid back in the same way. The wheel of fate may grind slowly, but I have seen it time and time again that the law averages makes its mark.

What you are and what you become are two different issues. You can have someone who comes from a good and loving background turn out bad. I believe that a bad upbringing can be the result of going one way or another. Love is so very vital, especially at the beginning of a child's life.

The Epigram of Freiherr Friedrich von Logau, as translated by Longfellow, states that "Though the mills of God grind slowly, yet they grind exceedingly small. Though with patience He stands waiting, with exactness grinds He all".

I love my children. When I was in labor with my son, I had no one around to help me. Harry was hardly at home. Fortunately, I had my scooter and side car. My mother was in prison again. The contractions were coming more frequently, so I left a note to Harry to feed our two dogs and off I went on my scooter to Mary Abbots Hospital in Kensington, where I had been delivered.

Sister McVay could not believe I had come to the hospital, pregnant, about to deliver, on my own, on a motorbike. I was an unmarried mother, but I wanted my child despite the difficulties. Harry was not really a consistent, dependable partner and I knew we would not always be together as he had another woman. Although I had a bad labor, I produced a fine baby boy and named him David. I did not care about his father. I had my baby boy,'

Chapter 6

PREDICTIONS COME TRUE

More became interested in Madame Doreena's readings. She said that she doesn't know how she does it. She knows that some people are psychic or telepathic regarding their loved ones, but knowing the lives of strangers and telling them about it is something else.

She explained, 'I just have the ability. It's a gift. People come back, because I clarify what's in their lives and what the roads are to take. They make the choice. I met a woman who worked in television production and a job opportunity came up. I had forecast that it would, and told her that it would not be good to take because it would result in a feud. The job came up, the situation occurred just like I said it would, and she came back to thank me.'

Doreen said that an Indian man once came to her and said that his brother-in-law had seen her do a reading. The Indian man asked, "How do you do it?" Apparently, the brother-in-law had told Doreen that he had two children, and she told him that he only had one. They argued about it. As it happened, a child died, after the man had come to see Doreen. She had only seen one child in his reading.

She credits her Spanish Rommany Gypsy family background and her Celtic heritage, from her father's side, for her psychic ability. 'The Celts were very mysterious,' she said, 'I have a bit of that as well as psychic ability inherited from the Spanish Rommany Gypsies.'

True to her ancestry, Doreen enjoys visiting Mallorca, an island off the coast of Spain, from time to time to meet with fans for Tarot and palm readings. Mallorca is a secluded tourist island off the coast of Spain with visitors from Spain, Germany and England. Movie stars Michael Douglas and his wife, Catherine Zeta Jones, have an estate there.

SANDY'S MUM

Doreen said, 'Everything I told her came true. Predictions were: June 1985, your situation has gotten worse over the years. It will get better. There would be a divorce. Someone was afflicted. Official papers, change job, documents/court, family getting back together – the girls, not her husband. You may have two jobs. Money will be better. Things thrown over the balcony, happened in relation to her separation from her husband.

Someone died at sea; necktie silk, possibly red, you are biding time to do things that you have always wanted to do. Definite break; you will move, go to Yorkshire. Danger/someone had rage. Car crash, Injury on foot, Coin collector, you are more in control of things now. New people are coming into your life.' Sandy's Mum wrote these notes and put stars beside the notes that came true – all stars.

GERTRUDE

Doreen said, 'At the time of her first reading, I saw a dark-skinned man in her life. I warned her that if she married this man, she would regret it, as he was very unpredictable and had a negative side to his nature. I could see

72

him in one of these moods, kicking a door.'

Gertrude put her fingers to her mouth, in surprise, and said, he did that two days ago. She was engaged to him at the present time.

Doreen said, 'I told her that he suffered from fits. I told her that she would regret marrying him, and to watch out for another bout of violence. I told her that that last bout of violence would help her make the decision to break off the relationship.

'A few months later Gertrude came back for another reading and told me that the bout of violence had happened, and that she had broken off the relationship. I was most relieved for her. As it turned out, he had behaved almost the same with another girl, and had since been in trouble with the police and ended up in prison.

'At another reading, I told her that two men and two women would be going away together. And once they were there, one of the men would meet another woman, and leave the woman he was with, and go off. There would be tears, anger and upset. Gertrude came back and told me that this had happened, but it was not her, but the other girl she went with and her boyfriend.   He did go off and meet another girl.

'At one reading, I asked Gertrude, do you know anything about all of these different colored bottles?   Some are green, some are brown, some are white, and all shapes and sizes, on the floors on the shelves on the table, everywhere. At that time, Gertrude did not know what I was talking about.

'Several months later, she told me what had come to pass about these bottles.   Gertrude had been to see a friend of hers, and when she went into the home and kitchen, she was amazed to see all of these bottles everywhere, all different sizes, shapes and colors, on the table, floor and shelves.

'Apparently her friend's brother's hobby used to dig up bottles from the earth wherever he traveled. He washed the bottles and added them to his collection.   Gertrude told me that her friend thought she had gone mad when she shouted out, "The bottles, the bottles, just like Doreen said".'

OLIVIA

First reading – I couldn't get any future on this reading; most of it was past and present. That happens sometimes. I don't know why. What I discussed were mostly past situations she could account for. The second reading a while later did not go well either.

At the third reading, I told Olivia that her future was now spread out, happening, and that she would not be back to see me ever again. You could not blame her for the look of disbelief on her face. I could see a crowded room, with mostly all the males on one side and the women on the other. A man noticed her, but would bide his time before talking to her.

She would move away from her friends to get a drink. Upon this move, the man would leave his friends and go to her side and chat her up. I described what he would be wearing – a brown coat. He would have a foreign name but would not speak the language. He would have a scar on his face at the hairline. He would come to pick her up to take her on a date in an expensive car and would give her a diamond ring, and she would marry him. All this came to pass, but she did not notice the scar on his forehead at first. His surname is Bercosi, and he is Italian, but he does not speak the language.

FATE IS FATE

When I begin a session with my client, especially if they have never had a reading before, I do explain that I do not tell them about their death, I do not tell them about any tragic future event. If I could change every bad situation, I would, but I can't. Fate is fate.

I have had a few clients who had troubled readings from other sources, and I had to unravel their worries. I see events where I tell them what could benefit them.

I have had similar readings. Some have been more outstanding than others. The shepherd must tend his sheep. This is the obligation that I am given after the negative meets the positive. Life has been given to us all, whether we want it or not. But life becomes so complex for some people. They lose their way and move aimlessly along, making one dreadful mistake after another, just like I did. I was faced with nearly every bad encounter but some invisible force stirred me away from trouble.

REFLECTING ON MY OWN LIFE

Yea, though I walk through the valley of the shadow of death, I will fear no evil. It is now that I realize that the trials for me were meant to be. I had to be given a taste of all the negative emotions to make me what I am today, not only for myself but for the many people who come to me to have their lives sorted out. Please, I am not a god or a saint or a martyr. I have just been given a gift to help others, of any nationality or religion.

CONNIE

She came to me when I lived in Morden. She has had many readings with me. So, over the years, I have come to know her. But I must tell you that when a person comes to me for a reading, I do not want to know anything about them whatsoever. They have come for me to tell them their future. They must not tell me what has happened or is happening. They may ask me questions after the reading, if they want to.

This was her first reading she ever had. I cast her cards and, oh dear, what a mess. Her present and future were utterly terrible. I told her so. She had someone in her life who was unpredictable. For her to get anywhere with her life, she must first cast him out of her life. I told her that it would take three years to have any improvement at all; that's how bad I saw her situation.

I remember throwing my hands up and telling her that I could see another bad encounter that would be coming up any day, a violent scene, broken glass all over, and that someone was going to be running through the glass in their bare feet, would be cut badly, and would not be able to walk for three or four days, or maybe even a week.

I told her that I could see her going from one place to another with her bags packed. I told her that she would seek safety, and although she would rid herself of this man, she would have trouble from him for several months after. Then, she would have family problems to sort out.

I told Connie that, eventually, she would get herself sorted out. I predicted that happiness would come from a heavy-set, fair man who would come into her life, and with whom she would settle down.   Everything I told Connie happened. The fair man came into her life and she is with him today. Her life at this moment of time still has problems, but she now has control.

HOW DID I GET TO THIS POINT?

What about her own trials and how she survived them? The reason she can help others is because of what she has inside her. Doreen's answer is lack of love, lack of love to the child is what is wrong.

She said, 'I went through my childhood and youth without love, like a boat without water. I had a helluva lot of problems, met with indifference.   No guidance at all, when you're crying out for love.

'As a baby. I was hospitalized, then home for a short time from the hospital. After that came the War and the evacuation of children from London. I lived with strangers and hundreds of other children, many handicapped children. The last place was the worst: Peckforton. It wasn't my Mum's fault that there was a war and that the children were moved far away into country-side homes. When I was returned to London at the age of 10, I found out that I had a half-brother from my Mum's marriage.

Polio patients, particularly children, did not receive the medical care they needed because of the need for doctors at the front. We were left in splints, but they don't do any good for you. Because of that, I realized that if I were going to have a splint on my leg all of my life, I would not be able to accomplish anything. That was the most miserable time of my life.

I WENT TO SCHOOL UNWASHED

Going around unwashed is dreadful; running around the neighborhood in your underclothes. That's what I did. I didn't know any different. No consistency or any pattern. As a teenager in school in London, I was always in trouble. I was rebellious, but I had a sense of justice. I used to get in trouble at school because of the lack of what I had.

I found it in myself to help other kids. When a kid was bullied at school, I would stick up for that kid, against the bully. I got into terrible trouble once. There was a big girl bullying another girl, calling her names and hitting the girl. I said, 'Don't do that. She's not hitting you'. The girl started on me, and she was bigger than me. So I took my belt off – because she was really pounding me with her fists – and I slashed her in the face. It's a lot of trouble I was in. The little girl whom I helped wouldn't come and help me. But I fought for justice.

Give me a comic to read or give me a book, and you would have a very easy-going girl. Once at Queensboro School, where Sister Tucker was the medical governor, she had charge of serving the dinner. I was reading this comic, nothing could shake me off. Dinner is around 12.

Somebody was talking, so she rang the bell, and said, 'Whoever is talking, we will stop dinner until that person stops talking'. It wasn't me. I put the comic under the table. She came up to my ear and rang that bloody bell in my ear, and I was furious, because it wasn't me. I pulled my chair from the table and said in a loud voice, it wasn't me. I have been reading my comic for the last half hour.

I got the blame and they said I was naughty. She rang that bell in my ear again, and I went berserk. I chased her all over the place, around the tables where the little kids were – I must have been 12 or 13 – and she was scared. Getting into trouble was easy for me.

MY APPETITE

I always ate every bit of dinner, always had an appetite, and went back for more. One day I went up, and it was custard, but one teacher was patient with me. She must have known something. But there was someone else who hit me on the head with the ladle – and it was a big ladle, because I asked for more. If I ask for more, it's because I am hungry. I said if there's more in that dish, give me more. She didn't want to give me any more. I was so angry that I lost my temper. I grabbed the ladle and put it in the custard, and the custard flew everywhere and we were covered in custard.

GETTING AWAY FROM MY FAMILY ENVIRONMENT

As a young woman, I was going downhill rapidly. I was mixing with bad people. I was promiscuous. I was like a ship without a rudder. I had no direction. I went from one relationship to another. At some point I began to realize that I was doing the same thing as my mother. That's the pattern. I saw it, in time. I was copying my mother: boyfriend after boyfriend. I had decided that nobody's was ever going to love me.

I had no self-confidence. If I went into a place, and didn't know anyone, my face was straight, I was worried. It was only after I had my children that I turned my life around. I finally realized, it's about my children. One child was put in a home. I was living with a violent man who beat me. Nobody knows what someone is going to be like until you are living with that person. I said to myself, what are you doing? I have shit in my life now, and if I don't get out, I will have shit in the future.

I got rid of my "husband", because my children were going to suffer. I showed them the love that I didn't have.

I changed overnight, got rid of the old man, just a nasty bit of work.

If someone is not good to you, you don't know any different. You have to learn the hard way. And I learned. My psychic ability was there, from the beginning. But I didn't know how to rely on it yet.

WANDLE TRAIL access guide became a reality for the disabled because of Merton Association for Independent Access (MAFIA). From left: the Mayor of Merton, Councilor Slim Flegg, Honorary Mayoress Doreen Ingram, and MAFIA members Pam Jones and Bob Wilcocks. They are shown in Morden Hall Park for the launch of The Wandle Trail access guide, which improves access to a local nature trail along the Wandle River. Merton is a historic site because William Morris founded his business along the Wandle River in the 1800's. He believed that the river had the best water for creating dye for fabrics such as chintzes.

Chapter 7

LOOKING FOR MARCASITE

I worked in the jewelry business. Once when I was planning to go on holiday in Europe countries, our boss asked us to look for Marcasite stones for his business. Marcasite could be found in Germany, particularly Oberstein, or Slavic countries.

Marcasite came into popularity during the reign of Queen Victoria who wore Marcasite in lieu of diamonds. Marcasite jewelry has a vintage look and was worn as an imitation of diamonds in the late Victorian era and the Art Nouveau/Edwardian period in England. Marcasite jewelry also was used in Greece and by the Inca Indians in South America.

Nellie and I set off for Europe. We boarded the train in Germany for a four-hour journey to Oberstein. We were on our way to see a Jewish lady, can't remember her name.

All of a sudden the train stopped and turned after two hours and didn't go straight on anymore. I started feeling ill. A thirst came on me. Nellie went and got me a glass of water. I still felt ill. The train stopped again. We were getting near the border, close to where we had to go. Then I started feeling alright again.

We had supper at a place in Oberstein, and we were telling the lady there about it. She got out a map and looked at it, and said, "This could be the explanation. It's a three-hour journey nearly going into Poland. When the train turned, it was on the Belsen track where they took the Jews in boxcars to the crematoriums in the concentration camps during the Holocaust".

I felt ill on the Belsen track that had taken people away in boxcars. When the train left that location, I was fine. That was weird.

During my jewelry career, looking for Marcasite, I enjoyed meeting with Polish people – djen dobja – I like the Polish people. They're great people. I feel sorry for the Polish people – they had the Germans on one side and the Russians on the other during two World Wars.

MY NEIGHBOR, RON

Doreen's story would not be complete without mention of Ron Bellamy her neighbor in Raynes Park, whom she loved calling "My Father", though he wasn't much older than her. Ron popped in every morning to bring Doreen a copy of the daily newspaper and to have a cup of tea.

Ron had lived at the same flat for 47 years, just a few doors away. He and his wife, Ida, were married 57 years. Ida died on holiday, after their 57th anniversary. Ida was in a wheelchair for 28 years, the result of a brain hemorrhage. He was 17 when they met.

World War II shaped lives and destinies. The only time that Ron and Ida were separated was during the War. He was captured in Germany with other British soldiers, near Leipzig and sent to a factory to work. He said that the Germans and Brits got to know each other and spent three years in the camp.

Ron said that he and his British friends were liberated from the labor camp by American soldiers on April 12, 1945, the day that President Franklin Delano Roosevelt died. American soldiers were crying. He said that he could not imagine British soldiers crying their eyes out if Churchill had died then. The Yanks told them, "You have to make your own way back. We're fighting a war and we have to go on".

Ron and the other soldiers crossed Germany. They stayed one night at a house with a German lady and moved the next night to a hospital full of German wounded.

They made our way to a hotel in Germany and we caught an American convoy to Brussels. From Brussels, they had a flight to England. They were released from the German labor camp on the 12th and Ron walked in the door of his home in London on the 18th.

He said, "My family did not know where I was and when or if I would ever return home". Ida said to him, simply, "Hello".

He had been missing for three years.

Ron said "After returning home to London, I worked with a firm that sold amplifiers and equipment for music production. Sir Paul McCartney used to buy mixers from us. My brother came out of a hospital eventually and joined Mega Dancing, in the 1950's, he used to run the business and booked the Beatles in the early days, when they were paid one pound 50 a night in the late 50's.

"Never knew my father. I might be the king of England, for all I know. I was pushed from pillar to post. First, I stayed a few months with an aunt, then another aunt. By the time I was eight, I had had eight homes. Cambridge, everywhere then my mother put me in Dr. Bernardo's home, for wayward children and I was fostered out. I still keep in touch with the daughter of my foster parents. They were lovely. I didn't know what it was to have a stable home, until I was fostered out."

"I lost Ida after 57 years of marriage. We were on holiday, our bags packed to come home, and Ida took sick. She died two days later. I had retired a year before our 57th anniversary, because the company went broke. It's still going, but the owner only has two people working for him and he works in his garage. Still provides amplifiers and other equipment for the rock groups.

"I Never went to America, was all around Europe. I went to Margate on the East Coast, in the summer. I still go there. When you're alone, and walking about on your own, you don't know what to do, it's no fun."

Ron Bellamy died in 2009.

PECKFORTON HAS A REUNION

I traveled to Chester and stayed at a bed and breakfast for the Peckforton Castle Reunion in 1992. In the courtyard with my elderly mother and childhood friends, I was overwhelmed with memories. I used to play whippintop in the courtyard. The water well and tables and benches are still there as well as the old oak tree, on a little hill. I used to stand there, watching the Yanks coming in lorries to visit the castle and put on a few good shows for the evacuee children housed in the castle.

The old Chapel was there, too. That was where I had a nosebleed, was taken back to my dormitory and the cloth was put over my face by the cruel helper who was in charge of the handicapped children.

Ms. Jessica Thomas, the administrator, had written about the evacuee children in her book, "Help for the Handicapped". Ms. Thomas did not mention the abusive treatment of one of her teachers.

At the 1992 reunion, I went around peering at all the girls' faces looking for recognition. For the most part, I couldn't remember the faces, but I remembered the names. Apparently, most of us felt the same. We all went along in little groups up to the castle. The great hall was still there. I noticed that most of the rooms were not used.

I had a lovely dinner in the great hall but I was very tired after all the mixed feelings. I felt that certain people stayed away from that reunion. They wanted to forget their lives there.

My old friend, Megan, told me that, as an evacuee child, she also had been roughly handled by the same teacher, dragged along with her knees bent. She suffered terrible pain. I remember that Megan had difficulty walking. She walked with her knees bent. I was amazed to see her walking now. She could stand tall and walk with no difficulty.

'I believe that if we had had the medical treatment and corrective surgery we needed as children, I am sure that a lot of us would have been much better on our legs today. Megan was one of the few people whom I remembered and recognized, after so many years.

Chapter 8

PINK BASKETBALL, WHITE BIBLE AND BLACK WITCHCRAFT

I had a friend at work, Barbara, for whom I read the residue of tea leaves in her tea cup. I told her that I saw a pink rubber ball with two sticks on it that you hang on, and a white bible. You either received it or you are going to get it soon. She looked shocked.

She worked in another department. I was just reading the tea leaves for fun. I did not know what it meant, but it was significant. She told our co-workers that there was no way that I could have known what she was planning. Barbara went to her department and came back with a brown piece of paper, an order for a pink basketball and a white bible. She had ordered them that day.

I started reading tea leaves in the 1970's. Interpretations that I had, based on the formation of the residue of the tea leaves, used to come true. I was told by a psychic that if you use your psychic ability, you will help many people.

When you are a psychic and have a good record for accuracy, sometimes someone wants to challenge you, like the lady I will tell you about in the story about a black witch. On one occasion I truly encountered the forces of evil.

STARTING OUT AS A PSYCHIC

I was wild as a young woman, a true Romany Gypsy. However, I was reading the tea leaves with some accuracy. I wanted to know more about this unusual ability. I went to visit two mediums who were supposed to be good. One wasn't.

The other held my hand and said, my dear girl, you have all the gifts, the gift of a medium and clairvoyance. Then he told me something which summed it up. He told me that fame would come to me in a strange way, because of who I am. "It will come to you," he said. "You have to keep going, you have all the gifts. You can go as far as you want to go. You have the Del Santo Gypsy tribe around you."

THE WHITE MOUSE

Fame never has been my goal. My idea of someone who has achieved fame and deserves recognition is an elderly lady named Nancy Wake who died in 2011. I met her briefly while visiting the Old Soldiers Home where Nancy Wake lived. Nancy Wake was a spy for the British during World War II, known as the "White Mouse".

When I met her, Nancy Wake was a little bedridden lady in her 90's. The White Mouse is credited with strangling German soldiers with her bare hands and interrupting the enemy's railroad lines. I commented, to Nancy Wake's nurse, 'I wish she could have strangled more enemy soldiers'. Then I asked the nurse, with an accent, what country she was from. It was Germany.

PURSUING FORTUNE TELLING

My psychic ability was part of my life. I knew exactly what I was doing.

Word got out and I wound up with clients from all over, French, American, and Spanish. Some have come to consult me regularly, for years. I don't like people coming back too quick, having one reading right after another. That's not fair to them as your life's circumstances don't change rapidly.

There are all sorts of reasons why people seek a psychic. Some people fear, some are skeptics, some lose their way. Sometimes I see a lot of human misery in people. And that's why I continue as a psychic: to help them out of their misery. I have no prejudices. I see people from different races, cultures and walks of life. Everybody needs someone to show them the way and give them a little hope for the future.

There is no such thing as a perfect future. There is a better future. You can learn to be a lot stronger to make decisions and accept your life. Your life can be better in your future than in your past, particularly if you are pretty strict with your money.

LETTERS FROM LORETTA

Through the years, I have had many letters from clients. They particularly like to write to me to tell me that something that I have predicted has happened.

My client, Loretta, wrote me a letter and underlined the word "farm" in the letter. She said that a relative passed away on July 9, beautiful funeral, and she was traveling to see a farm. I had told her, in a reading, that someone in the family had a farm. She denied it. I said that there will be a cow and a goat. She later found out that there was a farm in the family. She went to visit the farm and send me a note about it. "Off to the family farm, on a lake".

There is another letter about going to Egypt: I had predicted that she was going to Egypt. It took three and a half years for that to happen. She wrote to me that what I had said came true. She was having such mundane readings when we first met. I told her that her life was going to change and she was going to be happy. Loretta said, "hmmm, yeah". I even told her that she was going to meet an American and there was going to be a question of his asking her to marry him, and whether she was going to go with him. I predicted that she would fall in love with Egypt.

I also told Loretta that there was another country that she would love more, and would go there -- Ireland. Loretta did go there. She wrote, "As predicted, my boyfriend and I have had a few tiffs about family and money matters, but I am happier than I have been in a long time".

Another letter confirmed my prediction that she would visit some islands, and one was so remote you had to go by fishing boat. I had told her that there would be a big romance with the American, but there will be a question mark about it. She sent me a card, "Dear Doreen, arrived safely, have been to many islands, enjoying myself. I have met the American you told me about and he invited me to America for a visit. Don't know if I will go. I expect that lots more will happen. Have lots more to see and do."

Her unexpected travels were the result of a twist of fate. Somebody was supposed to go on a trip and had a ticket they would not use and gave it to her. That's how she went. She had never planned to go to these places.

THE WHITE WITCH VERSUS THE BLACK WITCH

If I were to ask you, do you believe in white witchcraft and black witchcraft, what would your answer be? Because we have not experienced some things doesn't mean that they don't exist. Do UFO's exist? Are there intelligent beings on other planets?

I encountered the evil force of black witchcraft when I lived in a flat in Becket Close, an area with meadows, a railway line nearby and lots of trees. There was a certain woman who lived in the flats. I had heard about her. My daughter used to play with the woman's little girl. This woman had an altar in her flat to do black art.

The woman in question used to catch flies and take them home while they were alive and put pins through them. The children saw her do that. Her daughter and mine were the same age, about six years old. I told my daughter not to go over to her friend's house.

If my children misbehaved, I would tell them to pack it up, get themselves together. But this woman went further. She would come down and pick up her child by the hair, or take a shoe to the child. Once she left a shoe mark on the child's face. Everybody in the neighborhood was terrified by her.

One day she came to my flat, knocked on the door and asked if her daughter was there and I said no. She told me that she had heard about me. She said that she believed in black art as it was so much more exciting. She said, "You deal in white witchcraft and I deal in black art". Her eyes were dark, opaque. I told her that I would continue to believe in what I believed.

I need to explain something about white witchcraft: you do not do bad things to anybody, you seek to heal. My pentacle, that I wear, is the symbol of the white witch. That shows that you want to extend love to others. I recognize, however, that there is a cult of the black witch.

The pentacle is a tribute to love. Anybody who looks at me sees only peace, love and hope. The symbol of the black witch is horns.

Our relationship became a contest between her power and mine. She was determined to overpower me. I made her angry. I challenged her. My teenage son, David, came home and told me about his teenage friend being involved in sexual trysts with this woman. I believe that there are demons, to turn a good person. She had David's friend in her clutches a young boy, about 15, 16 – for her sexual pleasure.

My son had two gold rings, and said, look what she gave me. I said why did she give you these rings? He said because she likes me. I said, No, David, there is a motive behind this. You take them back. He told me that the woman gave him the rings to persuade his teenage friend to go back to her – back into her clutches. She said to David, if I give you these gold rings, would you get him back for me?

David said that he didn't want to take the rings back because she wouldn't like it. I said, well I don't like it, and it is much more important that I don't like it than she doesn't like it. She is getting on my territory, using you, poaching my territory. You will take these back, and tell her that I don't want you to have these rings because these are not the right reason for you to have these rings.

I put the gold rings in an envelope and told David to take the gold rings back. I didn't want the gold rings in my flat. He took the gold ring back to her. This was a turning point.

A few days later, my little girl came home, crying her eyes out. The woman had frightened my six-year-old. I said to my daughter, don't worry about this. I know what's happening. I also told her little friend that I knew what was happening, and I wasn't blaming the little girl.

Tell your mother, if she's trying to frighten me, she can't frighten me with anything she does. After that, I didn't want my children going to that woman's home. It was too much for this woman, the idea that I opposed her. She was freely walking around the meadows, always upsetting someone, hurting someone.

Coming on a weekend, my door was always ajar so the kids could come in. But after half past eight, I had my door bolted, shut. All of a sudden, one Saturday evening, the locked door went flying open with a whooshing sound. She came flying into my flat. The funny thing about it was that I wasn't frightened. She would have given some other person a heart attack.

She called out, "Where is she?", in this dreadful voice. I was sitting in the front room. I told her that that was no way to enter someone's home. The right thing to do was to knock.

She said, "I have things to say to you that you won't like. You think you have power, my dear, but by the time I am finished with you, you will be finished." I wasn't frightened, that is what is so strange. She was standing by the door. She told me that I was going to be destroyed by fire. She said that I should not dare oppose her because of her power. What could I say? Alright then, whatever you are going to do to me, do it. Destroy me by fire, if you're going to do it. She was talking to me in symbols, and pointed, indicating the ground. It's not good, the symbol of the devil. In witchcraft, it means the devil on you. She was making symbols with her fingers and talking unintelligibly, I don't know what language, sounded like she was calling up the devil.

All she did for a living was to make people's lives miserable. I don't know where she got the little girl. I guess that she was married and all that. She told me that she knew that I had power, and I said if I've got power, I have enough to oppose you. You will not destroy me. Black magic destroys. White magic binds.

Suppose that you say something bad to me, like I hope you get hit by a coach. I am not allowed to say to you, with white magic, that I wish the same to you: I hope you get hit by a coach. In white magic, I bind you, so you can't do it to me. In white magic, I use a binding spell, so whatever you are going to do to me, you can't do it.

She said, "I will destroy you, and I will destroy you by fire, you will see fire all around you". She said, "You will die".

I told her that it would not work for me. I can't stop your power, but I said by the time you get back to your house, you will never walk down this path again, you will never walk around. That's what I am going to do to you, I will bind you. I will bind you to your house. You will never get around to terrorize anyone. I said, get out of my house and never enter my house again.

Late on Monday, I was washing in the bathroom, twisting and turning the sheets.   I didn't have a washer. Suddenly, there were two fires, I could spell smoke. My house was burning, it was ablaze, my ceiling was black, the clothes were burned black, that was on a Monday. I wasn't burned. I put my hand on the burning sheets and did not get burned at all. I took the whole lot of sheets that were on fire and put them in the bathtub.

There was no explanation about what caused the fire. Nobody was there, nobody had struck a match. This event happened late at night. The door was locked, I was doing the sheets, two were white and one was blue.

The second fire was on a Wednesday. The fire was in the kitchen. That woman did not come to the flat. I did not call the fire department. I put the flames out. No one was hurt.

The third fire was on Friday, in my bedroom. I had a big bedroom with a Queen Cottage carpet. You open the door and see a chest of drawers and the electric fireplace. The front door to my flat was locked and bolted, about half-past nine in the evening. I walked down to the bedroom. The flat was an L shape. I looked in the doorway. When you turn your gas range on, very low, it's like a blue flame.

I was standing at the doorway to my bedroom and I couldn't believe my eyes. There was something like a giant gas ring on the floor. I remember looking at it. It must have been a circle, not an electric fire. I just stood there, stunned. A giant gas ring, the fire burned in a circle over the carpet, a black circle on a cream-colored carpet. What I saw was a lot of smoke and what appeared to be a whole circle of electric fire. A giant ring was burning the carpet, burned the color out, so there was a black circle. It was a cheap carpet. There was no explanation for the third fire, either. I never had a fire in my life. I did not have any burns on me. Nobody had a match, nobody was there. That was it. There may have been coincidence to the first two fires, but not the third one. I didn't call the fire department, wasn't hurt.

From that past Saturday, when I told her that she would be bound to her house, from that day, she became housebound. She was afraid of coming out of her house. She had agoraphobia and never walked the meadow again. Never saw or heard from her again.

When you think about what she said, there was fire all around me, in the front room and in the kitchen, fire all around me. She had the power, but it wasn't too good. She told me that she would destroy me. I didn't say I will destroy you in return.

I bound her with white witchcraft. It isn't physical binding; I stopped her from destroying me. If you wish something on me, you will destroy yourself. You won't put a spell on me, I will bind you to your house. I have no doubt that you can attempt to put a spell on me, but you won't destroy me, you will destroy yourself. The power of evil rules to a certain point, but the power of good is stronger than the power of evil.

I am still around, I am doing good for others, always will. She is still in her house, not coming out. You will read about my hairdresser friend in another chapter of this book. The hairdresser came to see me some time after the fires, frightened. She said, "Doreen, you told me the story about that woman who tried to bind you. You will never guess who is coming to her beauty shop, that woman's daughter, who asked if I would come to her mother's house to do her mother's hair because she has agoraphobia."

VELIA'S READING

Velia's reading also was about fire, and I warned her that she should be careful of fire. She wrote to me that one day shortly after, she was rushing out of my flat, running late,

Since the reading about being aware of fire, she was more careful about the potential of fire, checking for burning cigarettes and putting them out promptly.

Prior to leaving her flat, she went to the bathroom and again thought of Doreen's warning of a fire. She smelled fire, thought it was my imagination and was going to ignore it. She went into her bedroom, and in her rush to leave, she had left the space heater on and some clothes had fallen on the heater and were smoldering. She felt that if she had not been made aware of fire though her reading, she may not have noticed the faint smell and her flat probably would have burned down.

AN ENDORSEMENT FROM MARY

My name is Mary, and I have been coming to Doreen for quite a few years now. Doreen is about the best card reader I know. She is so accurate and has helped my life so much. For so long, all Doreen saw was dark clouds and hard times. She was right. But she also saw a good future ahead. At long last this is coming.

She also saw a female with a piece of gold. This turned out to be my mother-in-law who died this year. Doreen saw the death of a male that was unexpected, with lots of sorting out. That was my father-in-law who died soon after his wife. And there was so much sorting out of papers for two years.

We were nearly going to sell our house because of a lack of funds, and Doreen told me that something would save us at the last minute and that happened. Our home was saved. But the most outstanding of all is about my cat. I had a reading with Doreen when she stopped and said, 'The cat, the cat, the cat!'. Doreen said there was something about a cat meeting with an accident. I thought she meant Honey, my kitten, who had died some time back. When I arrived at home, my husband came out looking upset. I knew something had happened to our kitten named Peppy. At the very same time that Doreen was telling me about my cat, my Peppy was run down by a car.

DOREEN, A TRIBUTE TO A FRIEND OF MANY YEARS

One client wrote a poem about Doreen:

Appointment book tonight at eight
A special date, I can't be late
For an hour I will transcend
A special time spent with my friend.
I heard her wisdom for many years,

She knows my hopes,
My dreams, my fears.
She's known the past,
She's seen my pain,
The present now, my loss, my gain.
My future, too, she sees ahead

Interprets what the cards have said.
Sees what will and is and has been,
The tarot now will set the scene.
So many things have come all true
A mystery just how she knew

A precious gift, she holds the key
And opens up the inner me.
She has a very special power
And it unfolds within this hour.
With clear precision tells me more
Of loved ones who have gone before.

She sees the happy times ahead
She seems to know what's in my head.
I've gone with friends
For notes I've taken
Such clarity is not mistaken.

A crossroads shown sometime ahead
Unraveled now the tangled thread.
Fears are laid and with assurance
Warnings made well in advance.
An hour well spent in revelation –
I feel a sense of declaration.

When I leave I am uplifted
By one so wise and truly gifted.

ACCOLADES FROM JENNIFER

Doreen is a godsend, as far as I am concerned. I have been coming to her for two years now and her readings have helped me tremendously. They are so accurate that they are frightening sometimes. These are some of the things that Doreen told me and their outcome:

Doreen asked me if someone served a summons on me, at my home. I had been served a summons the previous day in connection with me being evicted from my home. This was the first summons I had ever had, and not an everyday occurrence. I did not tell anyone. She couldn't have known.

She said she could see someone in my family with a health problem and if it wasn't treated, surgery would be needed. Two months later, my father was admitted to the hospital with a malignant growth that was behind his ear, which had been threatened for more than six months.

She asked me if anyone had lost any important document like a birth certificate or a check book. Two months later, I needed my birth certificate to apply for a passport. Needless to say, it couldn't be found anywhere.

Doreen asked me if anyone had had a break-in, either house or car. Answer was no. She said, somebody would, but they must get insurance before it happened. On returning home, my father told me that the night before, his office had been broken into. Typewriters and computers had been stolen. He was not insured.

Doreen told me that she could see me traveling abroad. This was a complete surprise to me, as I had nothing planned and it was financially impossible.   But sure enough, three months later I was at a nightclub and I won a weekend trip to Malta.

These are only a few things that have happened. Doreen tells you exactly what she sees. Her readings are by far the most accurate I know.

Chapter 9

THE STORY OF FABIENNE

Fabienne was an attractive fashion model. Fabienne had readings about her career and her love life. She traveled in glamorous social circles in Great Britain and Europe. She came to see me whenever she was back in London, after photo shoots out-of-town. Fabienne had readings about her career, particularly her love life.

One time when she came, she was most surprised at the reading. I told her that her cards were very bad. I didn't like her cards. They were laid in a bad order. I told her to be careful. She asked me to explain it. I told her that there is a dark man whom you know. This is a handsome man from a foreign country with dark eyes and a dark complexion. Be very careful, because he is going to ask you to go to his country and you are going to go. Fabienne said that she didn't know what I was talking about.

I told her that she didn't know at the time of the reading, but it would all become clear very soon. I warned her that she would travel with him to his country and he was going to trap her in his flat. She wasn't taking notice of my warning because it didn't make any sense at the time. I went on and told her, "You're going to stay in his flat. For the first three days it is going to be lovely because he will be Prince Charming. He will charm you.

"After three days, you will feel uneasy and want to leave. He is not going to like that because he is too controlling. He is going to lock you in the flat. He is a businessman, and he will go out to work each day, and leave you locked in his flat every day".

She looked at me like I was crazy. I said, 'Fabienne, please listen. I am so worried about this man. But the good thing that I am going to tell you is that you are going to get out. This is what is going to happen: you are going to have an argument because you want to leave and he doesn't want you to leave.

'Here comes Mr. Bad Man. He is going to backhand you, and you are going to slither down the wall. That is when you are going to remember me. You will remember your reading, the reading I am giving you now. You are going to say these words, as you slide down the wall, "This is what Doreen was talking about". You will know that you will get away, because I told you that you would. At the end of the week you will get out.'

It happened. Fabienne met someone and went with him to his home country in the Mideast. At first, the boyfriend was charming . . . until Fabienne wanted to leave. Doreen continued, 'He slapped her and, like I told her, she slid down the wall and remembered my words. He kept her locked up in the flat. Each day, he went to work – business as usual.

'In the interim, while locked up, Fabienne collected her belongings in a bag and prepared to get out. She still didn't know how she was going to get out of his flat. In my reading, I had told her that she was going to get out of this flat and that she was going to come back and tell me about it.'

A few months later after the reading, Fabienne rang me after she had been away on an assignment. She said, "I have something to tell you – amazing – everything you told me on that last reading happened. I did leave the country with this man and wound up locked up in his flat when I told him that I wanted to leave. He took my passport away from me. I am grateful that I came to see you and had that reading because it helped me to get out".

Fabienne did not know how she was going to leave and waited for an opportunity to present itself. One day the boyfriend returned to his flat from work and rushed to the toilet. First, he put his briefcase down on the table. Fabienne flew into the briefcase, found her passport, took her bag that she had packed and fled. She returned to England.

ANIMALS IN HER PREDICTIONS

I love all animals, including the stray fox that comes to my back porch to be fed, cats that find their way into home and all other animals. I hold the designation of Leadership Supporter for the IFAW, International Fund for Animal Welfare. I regularly give donations to the Blue Cross Animal Hospital to help animals that have been rescued. It is natural that animals are included in my readings. I put out dog food for the fox that comes to visit nightly and it's gone by the next day. I have named the fox Wendy. Wendy blows me a kiss now and then.

OFFERING HOPE

In her bedroom I keep a box of letters from clients, people for whom I have done readings and who have written to me, astounded that what I predicted happened. I am always happy to hear that I have given hope to someone. One letter that I received was from Elizabeth who, I recall, grabbed my hand after a reading and said, "You have given me the inspiration to live". Elizabeth's letter was dated April, 1996

"You have given me hope. I had completely given up on everything. I was beginning to believe that I was never to have happiness and contentment in my life, always to struggle and to lose. Meeting you was a valuable experience and an honor".

REBECCA, THE HAIRDRESSER

Rebecca was a great hairdresser – that's how we met. She fixed my hair. Rebecca came to see me for readings about her love life. I saw that her marriage would break up and told her that, Even if she tried to make a go of it, by September it would be over and her life would go into a new direction. I also told Rebecca that she would move, and she did.

Rebecca had another reading, and I asked her, 'What have you been doing with black shoes? They are unusual, and you can't buy these shoes in an ordinary shoe shop'. I did not know that, two days previously, Rebecca had arranged to take flamenco dancing lessons. She tried on a pair of flamenco dancing shoes and bought them.

At the same reading, I kept getting signs of a heel and a toe. It turned out that this was a method used in a flamenco dance that she was learning at the time. I walked with difficulty most of my life and now I am confined to a wheelchair. Dancing lessons were never an option, however, that did not

119

interfere with my lifelong love of music and the theatre.

REBECCA IS CHAUFFEUR-DRIVEN

To Rebecca's surprise, at one reading I told her that she would be sitting in the back of a Rolls Royce. Three months later, Rebecca met a man who wined and dined her. Every time they went out on a date, she was always picked up in the chauffeur-driven car.

REBECCA'S BOYFRIENDS

Rebecca was very pretty and attracted boyfriends. I told her that she would meet a man who would be very rich. "Never mind about his big nose", I said, "just think about what he wants to do for you and spend on you". I also mentioned that she would be invited to take trips to Paris and there was someone of Jewish religion involved. About a month letter, she met a prominent businessman who happened to have a large nose, and who did invite her to travel to Paris.

In another reading, I told Rebecca that she would meet a man who had a drug problem, and she would know about it. I told Rebecca to be careful, as she could get involved in something dangerous, but this man would go from her life as quickly as he came.

Five weeks after this reading Rebecca met a man who answered the description in my reading, and with whom she started to become emotionally involved. It was clear from the start that he depended on drugs, heroin, and cocaine. Unbeknown to Rebecca, he was also involved in drug-smuggling. Her tarot card had shown a man surrounded by bad cards, which also meant that he was involved with people of bad influence.

Rebecca's reading consisted solely about this man who was in her life at that time. I saw two directions for him, one was to give up drugs and never be involved and live freely, and the other was disaster and financial ruin and possibly death. It also mentioned that he would have a legal document, probably a will, to sort out.

Shortly after this reading, this boyfriend's parents died, first his mother and later his father. Rebecca's boyfriend was in no fit emotional state to deal with the wills that they had left. He told Rebecca that he was going abroad to sort out these legal problems. As I had told her, he went out of Rebecca's life.

In a later reading, I told Rebecca that a woman was the reason why this man had gone so suddenly from her life. Several months later, a woman informed Rebecca that her boyfriend had gone abroad on a drug mission and all the people around him were caught and imprisoned. He escaped getting caught, but could never enter this country again.

MORE REBECCA READINGS

Doreen said, 'In another reading, I was amused to relate to Rebecca that she would be in a pub and would turn around and notice a man with funny hair. I told Rebecca that he would be wearing a toupee, and she must not start laughing. That very night, Rebecca was in a pub with a friend, and exactly as I had predicted, Rebecca turned around and saw a man next to her with an orange-colored toupee. Rebecca later told me that she nearly choked on her drink.

At another reading, I saw a chair which needed to be repaired. Rebecca could not relate anything to a chair. Then a few days later she came to my flat to do my hair. I sat down on a chair, but suddenly I said to Rebecca, 'Shall I change to another chair?' Rebecca said, "No, that one will be alright." The chair collapsed just as I saw on the seat. It collapsed amid laughter, and with the hairbrush caught up and dangling in my hair. Only my dignity was damaged.

Chapter 10

FALSE FRIEND

I became close friends with a certain person at work. I used to go out to pubs with her and her husband and I thought that she was my friend. Apparently she didn't reciprocate the friendship. Her husband was very good to her, and then there was me, on Social Security, very poor, with three kids. For Sunday dinner, I used to go with my friends to a pub. It was a gay club and we enjoyed the entertainment, with the drag artist.

I have no inclinations. I wasn't interested in gay women who occasionally tried to came on to me. I am a universal person, who likes everybody and I take an interest in people. Even though I was very poor, I used to pay my way.

DIRTY TRICK NO.1

The first dirty trick that my former friend played on me was when I was just coming up to having a bit of money and it was my son's birthday. I thought that I would like to buy him something nice for his 16th birthday.

At that time, someone we knew was showing us a box of coins, medals and things like that; they were going on the cheap. He showed them to me and my friend. He asked me if I wanted to buy something, and I saw one that would be just the right nice little coin for David, my son.

I thought it was the best thing that I could buy for David, because we were so poor. I asked the seller to please hold that coin for me and when I was paid at the end of the week, I would buy it.

Of all the coins that there were, when it came to Friday, and I went to buy the coin, he told me that my friend already bought it. Of all the coins, she could have bought the next one up, as she had more money than me. That was a dirty trick. I said nothing to her about it.

DIRTY TRICK NO. 2

Then, another event happened where my friend and I worked at a mail market. I used to get extra money by doing what we call a cutout. I took the printout home over the weekend to work on it. I was a sorter, and knew all the characters for England, Scotland and Wales. I used to sort out all of the addresses for the mailing and then other employees used to stuff enclosures, such as brochures, in the envelopes.

Sometimes a cutout would come, and it would have things stuck together, so I would separate the counties on it. It was worth 20 pound to me every month.

There was a crew, about six of us doing the sorting. They were all married, happily married. I was the only one on my own, bringing up three children by myself. None of them wanted to do the cutout work over the weekend.

I took the cutouts home with me and did them to make extra money. When I went up to my boss on one occasion, for my wages, he told me that my friend had already seen him and had taken the cutout, for which I always earned the extra 20 pounds.

My friend told me later that, since she learned, presumably, that I was going out for the weekend and I wouldn't be able to do the work. My boss gave the cutout for extra money to her. That was the second dirty trick.

I didn't see my friend for five days after that, but the following weekend we made it up to go to the pub. She brought along a friend, Ella, who instantly didn't like me. I asked her to not bring Ella to the pub again when I was in the party.

At the time, I had a second cousin from New Zealand come over, very naïve, not sophisticated in the ways of life. She stayed with me for a few weeks before she found a job in London.

I continued to go to the pub for Sunday dinners with my friend and her husband. We always had nice evenings. On one occasion, we were all at the pub when my friend pointed out a handsome man standing next to me. I was not impressed; I don't run after men and didn't go to the pub to meet.

I took a notice. I turned around to look, and thought he was handsome, wearing a lovely tweed, smart-looking. While we were laughing about whoever was on the stage, he introduced himself. He said that his name was Lester and he came from Essex Way, Newtown.

'He said, I've not seen you here before – I come up every week to see my Mum who lives nearby and I pop in here. He said, would you like a drink?'

I said I was with company, and it would be rude to disassociate myself from them. He asked me if I would go out with him sometime and I gave him my phone number.

Lester and I became close friends. We went out together for the next several months each time that he was in London. When he came up from Essex, he went to visit his mother, and then he used to come into the pub and give me a kiss. He used to get my key, go for a take-away, and we would go back to my place.

My friend always asked, "How are you getting on with Lester?" I said, 'Fine'.

One day, I made it up to go to the pub with my co-worker and her husband. I said to my little cousin visiting from New Zealand to join us.

I told my cousin that I was getting ready in the bathroom, and I would be ready soon. There was a knock on the door. I said that would be my girl friend. Who was on the doorstep was my friend and Ella, the girl with whom I didn't want to go out with my friend.

I straight away knew it was a set-up. I told them to wait in the front room for me, and then we would go to the pub. I told my cousin, Alice, that that girl is here for a reason, because she doesn't like me and I don't like her. Ella is coming with us to take the boyfriend away from me. Alice said, "Doreen, No!"

I predicted that we would be standing in the pub, Alice, my girl friend, her husband and Ella, in a circle. I told Alice that Lester would come in later on. He would kiss me and take the key. We usually went out somewhere or he waited for me at the pub.

What's going to happen is that Lester is going to come in, he's going to kiss me, and buy us all a drink, and say, "See you later, Love. I will wait for you to come home, perhaps we will have a Chinese or go out". When he comes in, Ella will move around, I will be talking to someone else, and Ella is going to move close to Lester and chat him up.

That is what happened that evening. And Doreen's cousin noticed. Alice said, "Look, Doreen, Ella's moving around, just like you said". Lester kissed me, took the key, left the pub and waited for me to come home.

The next day, my friend rang me up on a Saturday, which is something she never did. She said, "How did you get on with Lester last night?" I said, "Fine, we had Chinese and stayed in". My friend said, "I have something to tell you – he has Ella's phone number and he is going to take her out". I said, 'Is he? Well, I am going to tell you something. I knew all about it, all about your set-up. Do you that I didn't know what you were doing? As soon as I saw you there with Ella, I knew it was a set-up. From now on you are no friend of mine. That's the third dirty trick you did to me. I don't want to see you again. You're not a friend.'

She started crying. I said, 'Do you know what's going to happen to you? For the three dirty tricks you played on me, you're going to get them back. You're going to get a return. I don't want your friendship, I don't need you. What you put out in this world you get back in return, whether it's good or whether it's evil. You're going to get it back.'

By the way, Lester did not take out Ella.

I didn't see my friend and her husband again; no more phone calls, no more Sunday dinners at the pub. I dropped her. After five years. Why did she take the coin from me? She denied me the coin, she denied me the cutout, and she denied me Lester. Lester told me all about it.

About a year after the incident in the pub, the phone rang, and a very croaky voice came on the phone, I said, 'Who's that?' It was my former friend. She told me that she was ill and asked me to come to see her.

I had forgotten about my friend and her dirty tricks. I had completely put her out of my mind. I went to see her and she was sitting up in a chair, and she said, "What more are you going to do to me?

"You said three things are going to happen to me. Here's one of them -- I just had my gall bladder taken out. My husband lost his job that he had worked at for many years. Then we lost the chance to buy the house we were living in".

She cried. She said, What more are you going to do to me? Please, there's no more, is there?" I thought to myself, "Strange things come from me".

WHAT GOES AROUND COMES AROUND

There was a woman who worked at the shop who used to always get on my back, reporting me to the office. I barely knew this woman. I didn't know what this woman was about. One day the manageress came to see me and told me that T. had reported me. I asked him what for. He said that I put the addresses underneath the box.

We had been told to clear up the rubbish because we had clients coming in. I put the address labels underneath a box. This woman kept her eyes on me all the time. I put the labels under the box for safety's sake because if we sweep up the floor, the labels would be swept up.

That was on a Friday. Lucia came up to me and told me that T. still wanted a go at me. I said, 'Do you know what's going to happen? That lady is going to fall down and break her leg, and she won't be coming to work for a couple of weeks or maybe months.' I was so angry.

Monday came, and Lucia came to me with a struck look on her face. "Doreen, I have something to tell you. You know T.? She fell and broke her leg and she won't be in". I thought she was making it up. I said, 'You're joking, don't joke about that'. Lucia said, "I'm serious, Doreen, I am so serious". I approached the manageress and said, 'Is that right about T.?' She told me that T. would not be coming to work for awhile.

There have been such weird things in my life, I don't want to boast. That's a true story.

A couple of years after that, my friend's husband died and she was alone. I think she was sorry – but she never ever said to me that she was sorry. I think she appreciates my friendship, I am still a good friend.

MESSAGES FROM THE OTHER SIDE

I am not a medium. A medium is someone who claims that he or she communicates with the spirits of people who have passed on but who have messages to share. In what is called channeling, mediumship works in two ways: psychics claim to speak to spirits and relay what they are told or else the channeler goes into a trance and is "possessed" by a specified spirit.

In America, mediums are met with much skepticism. However, at the University of Arizona there is a research program at the Laboratory for Advances in Consciousness and Health in the

Department of Psychology. The VERITAS Research Program, run by Gary Schwartz, was created primarily to test the hypothesis that the consciousness (or identity) of a person survives physical death. Britain takes telepathy a bit more seriously. The Society for Psychical Research investigates such phenomena mainly in connection with telepathy and apparitions.

One day, I was giving a reading to a lady named Martina. I did not know that Martina had been raised by her grandmother. During the reading, I told Martina that it felt as if a woman came to me and took over. I couldn't do the reading because this unknown woman just took me over/possessed me.

I told Martina that she had a black box and that all of her grandmother's pieces were in it. The box had a container in which you put false teeth. I told Martina that her grandmother wanted her to get rid of the items.

I had to talk to Martina with the aid of a Spanish interpreter as Martina did not speak English. The grandmother, who had literally taken me over, said that Martina had black lace and religious things. The grandmother said I am dead now, Don't save those things. Get rid of them. I don't need them anymore.

For that reading, I wound up being a medium, "taken over" by the deceased grandmother and I could not do the reading, The "spirit" said, "Stop it, Lolita is talking". Martina told me that Lolita was her grandmother's name. Martina said me that was always thinking about her grandmother and she loved her very much.

Chapter 11

MY ANCESTORS: THE ROMMANY GYPSIES

The Rommany Gypsies came to Turkey and Greece around 1000 A.D. but they are documented as being called "atsinganoi" or Gypsies from the Byzantine era when there was a famine in the ninth century. In 800 A.D., St. Athanasia wrote that he gave food to atsinganoi near Thrace. In 803 A.D., Theophanes the Confessor wrote that Emperor Nikerhoror I had the help of atsinganoi to put down a riot with "their knowledge of magic". Atsinganoi were referred to as itinerant fortunetellers, ventriloquists and wizards who visited Emperor Constantine IX in 1054 A.D.

A Franciscan monk, Symon Simeonis, in 1322 wrote an account of atsinganoi in Crete where they lived in oblong tents like Arabs and also in caves. In 1350, Ludolphus of Sudheim (maybe in Germany; "sudheim" is the Norse word for south home) discussed a similar people with a unique language whom he called Mandapolos, which was possibly derived from the Greek for mantes, fortuneteller. In 1360, according to historians, the Rommany founded in Corfu an independent principality called Feudum Acinganorum which was a settled community with an established economy.

The first Gypsies slipped into England very quietly. An anonymous writer in1612 states that they first began to gather in the south of England in the early 1500's. They had a king named Giles Hather and a queen, Calot. The vagabond element seems to have been developed in England and their dialect, old Cant, was based on Rommany.

In 1522 they were described as an outlandish people calling themselves Egyptians, exercising no craft but palmistry and robbery. In 1530, the first law was enacted to deport Gypsies from England. During the reign of Queen Elizabeth I, 1533-1603, it was suspected that Gypsies harbored Catholic priests and for some years a great persecution was carried on against them.

By 1549 they were included in a search made through Sussex for vagabonds, Gypsies, conspirators, prophesiers, players and the like. For whatever reason, at this time, Gypsies were imported into England. But a great number of them were returned to France. In 1554 England passed its first law that made being an immigrant Gypsy a crime, punishable by death. But by 1563, there were 10,000 Gypsies in England.

WHAT WAS WRITTEN ABOUT GYPSIES

In the 16th century, Spanish writer Miguel de Cervantes, of "Don Quixote" fame, called Gypsies "lords of the open country". William Shakespeare wrote about the Gypsies, stating that they "speak their own language". It is not unlikely that John Bunyan, the 17th century preacher and writer, was of Gypsy origin, as his father was a tinker, and Bunyan spoke of being of the most despised race in the land. John Ruskin, the 19th century naturalist and essayist who advocated the simple life, said of the Rommanys, "honestest, harmlessest of the human race".

A study of historical dates relates that in 1596, 106 men and women were condemned to death at York just for being Gypsies, but only nine were executed. The others proved that they were born in England. The last known execution for being a Gypsy was in Suffolk. Gypsies were often deported to the United States.

In 1749 the Spanish started their roundup of the Gitano's (Gypsies) that was a raid to separate families and put the able-bodied men into forced labor camps.

In the 1750's, Gypsies sold themselves as slave labor to reach Pennsylvania, which would become one of the original colonies of United States. The Gypsies in Pennsylvania formed a community known as the Chi-keners or "Black Dutch" and presumably their descendants still to be found in the United States. today.

GYPSIES IN HUNGARY

Child slavery thrived in Hungary in the 16th century: gypsy children sold for the equivalent of fifty cents. The persecution of Gypsies continued through the ages. From 1768-1782, during the reign of Marie Theresa, queen of Hungary and Bohemia, attempts were by government decrees to force Gypsies to settle. The decrees removed rights to horses and wagon ownership, forced Rommany boys into military service and prohibited marriage between Romannys. Queen Maria Theresa's successor, Josef II, prohibited the wearing of traditional Rommany clothing and the use of the Rommany language was punished by flogging. The 1782 census in Hungary of Gypsies counted 1,582 musicians among 43,787 Gypsies.

GYPSIES AND THE AMERICAN REVOLUTION

The American Revolution in the 1770's gave Gypsydom in England its greatest blow. Gypsies were forced in large numbers into the British fleets and armies serving in America. Most of them deserted, finding America a congenial home. Another blow to the tent-loving Gypsies was the British Enclosure Act, which ordered all commons and wastelands to be enclosed, thus depriving them of places to camp.

The first serious book, calling for better treatment of the Gypsies in England, was penned by John Hoyland, a Quaker, in 1812. There were some charitable projects as a result, but later many Gypsies were transported as criminals to Australia. Another innovation of the early 1800's was the first wooden horse-drawn caravan which was to become the Gypsies' iconic mode of transportation for more than a century.

It is estimated that a million Roma (Rommany Gypsies) live in America today. Gypsies first crossed the Atlantic with Christopher Columbus in 1492. Most Americans believe clichés about Gypsies that give them a bad reputation. Latin Americans, from Central and South America, who love Flamenco music may not realize that they are hearing Gypsy music.

GYPSIES IN ENGLAND

By 1874 there were only a few hundred full-blood tent Gypsy families in

England. There were about 20,000 Kairengroes, or house-dwellers, who keep their Gypsy blood a secret, and half-breeds, posh au post, or those affiliated by blood – all of whom possessed the great secret of the Rommany language to a greater or less degree.

During the European mass migrations of the 1880's to the United States, the Gypsies were denied entry to the U.S. and also some South American countries.

The British Children's Act in 1908 made it compulsory for Gypsy children to attend school, but only for half a year.

GYPSIES HOLOCAUST

The Nazis committed genocide against the Gypsies. The Gypsies throughout Europe were all but annihilated from 1935 to 1945 during the holocaust of World War II. Estimates are that up to 500,000 to 1.5 million Gypsies were killed in Europe. In fact, the Nazis drew up lists of English Gypsies for interment.

The persecution started in Germany in 1935 when the Rommany were denied citizenship and imprisoned in concentration camps. This precedent was followed in Croatia, Romania and Hungary. In Central Europe, the extermination of Rommany in Bohemia and Moravia was so effective that the Bohemian Rommany language became extinct.

When some Nazi expert on racial history discovered, towards the end of the WWII, that the Gypsies descended from common Aryan ancestors and was more unmixed than most European races, orders were given that no more should be sent to the gas chambers.

In Great Britain, during World War II, the British Government created caravan sites for families of Gypsies in the British army or doing farm labor. Those sites were closed after the War.

SCOTTISH GYPSIES

Tradition holds that the Gypsies were in Scotland in 1460. There is a curious little record, made by the Lord High Treasurer of Scotland, which was dated April 22, 1505: "To the Egyptians by the King's command, payment of seven pounds." That was a considerable amount of money at the time, possibly comparable to 100 pounds now. It must have been a payment either for something valuable or some service, and later inferences are that it was payment of the king's money for Gypsy entertainment: music, dancing, singing, and fortunetelling.

"Les Egyptians", as the French called them, caused great interest and curiosity. Royalty invited the Gypsies to their palaces to entertain and dance. Perhaps that's when the Gypsies engaged in their practice of relieving the gaujos (non-Gypsies) of various possessions, of which the Rommany Gypsies felt they were entitled. Folklore has it that the Gypsies were given a divine right to steal by Christ as they had stolen the nails to be used in the Crucifixion in an attempt to prevent it.

In 1566, James IV granted them a letter of favor, based on the premise that they were true penitents of Egyptian descent. When the Gypsy king was informed later that it was time for him to leave the country and end his pilgrimage, presumably "commanded by the pope", he said that he had been robbed by some of his subjects.

Tradition also holds that James V, while traveling in disguise, was treated cruelly by two Gypsies of a band of three, in consequence of which he made a law that whenever three tinkers or Gypsies were found together, two should be hanged and the third set at liberty. This order was in force only one year, and the Gypsies were basically unmolested. After a period of peace, several edicts against Gypsies appeared in 1592, 1600, 1603 and 1609. Although it was a capital crime to be a Gypsy, and they were hunted down with excessive severity, they remained in great numbers.

In Scotland, Gypsies called themselves Nawken. A small town in the 1800's, Kirkyetholm, was at one time peopled by Gypsies, in consequence of a Gypsy, by his bravery at the siege of Namur, having obtained a grant authorizing his descendants to dwell there. Few Gypsies remain in Scotland, as great numbers of them went to America where they generally became house-dwellers and became lost to view.

GITANO'S IN SPAIN

Attempts were made to assimilate the Gitano's in Spain by 1619. The historic Spanish Inquisition singled out Jews and Gypsies during a period of religious persecution. The Gypsies were forcibly sedentarized, use of the Rommany language was prohibited and Gitano men and women were sent to separate workhouses and their children sent to orphanages.

CONTINUED RESHUFFLING OF GYPSIES

Depending on your source, estimates in 2010 are that there are 10 million or more Gypsies in the world. They are the fastest growing minority in Europe, with millions living in the Czech Republic, Slovakia, Hungary, Bulgaria, Romania and other countries. In the Czech Republic, the government is defying a European court order by continuing to place thousands of Gypsy children in schools for the mentally disabled, according to Amnesty International. This follows a pattern that was implemented in Norway when laws were passed to remove Gypsy children from their parents and place them in institutions. The result was that some 1,500 Rommany children were taken from their parents in the 20th century.

In France, in 2010, hundreds of Gypsies were sent back to their native Romania by the Government. The Gypsy camps were emptied and those Gypsies who were deported received a small stipend from the French Government to start anew in their home country. However, much like Mexicans deported in America, there is nothing to prevent them from returning to France in the near future.

TRADITIONS THAT HAVE BEEN LOST

At least one Gypsy historian says that Gypsies have a God-given right to beg, called mongering, especially clothing. Folklore has it that the two Mary Saints, Mary Salome and Mary Jacoby, fled Palestine after the Crucifixion of Christ. When the party arrived at a Provence fishing village, in the wild Rhone delta, it was Sara, the dark Gypsy servant of the women, who begged clothing and food from the fishermen and their wives, for the two saints. It is said also of Sara – Saint Sara of the Gypsies – that the boat left the shores of Palestine without the Gypsy. Upon hearing the lamentations of her loyal servant, Mary Jacoby cast her cloak upon the sea, and the Gypsy rode upon it to the boat.

Another tradition lost is that English Gypsies used to bury their dead in remote places, but later became careful to secure Christian burials. Their ordinary weddings generally consisted of nothing but an announcement and a feast, but in later years the better class retained a minister. Several Hindu superstitions not known to the English prevailed, such s the evil eye and a belief that the blindworm sees for half the year out of his right eye and half with his left. Like the Hindus, the Gypsies sent cooked food for three days to the family of a deceased person which was called by the Hindu term karwa khana.

GYPSY ROMA TRAVELLER ACHIEVEMENT SERVICE

Citing to the Gypsy Roma Traveller Achievement Service (GRTAS), Gypsy fairs in England are a lot more than a fun day. The Fair in Appleby-in-Westmoreland is the most famous of the Traveller Fairs in England and attracts people from all over the world every year in early June. The Charter was granted by King James II in 1685 for the sale of goods and cattle and now includes horses.

Lee Gap Fair is the oldest chartered fair in England, dating from 1136 A.D. Gypsies first went to the fair in the 1540's and have continuously supported the Fair where families meet every year. GRTAS states that the week of the Fair is one week when the Gorgio population is in the minority and the Gypsy culture and traditions are renewed from a historical perspective.

The Gypsies ride horses bareback and wash them in the River Eden before showing and selling them on Fair Hill. The deal is always done with a slap of the hand and cash. Songs, music and story-telling can be heard around camp fires. And there's peg-making, flower carving, wagon (vardo) building and painting, blacksmith and leather work and fortunetelling going on, too. You can buy a variety of goods – fine china, cut glass, pictures, furnishings, clothes, shoes, pots, horse-tack and music. The GRTAS cites to other Gypsy fairs in England, including Brough Hill and Yarm Fair in September-October.

Chapter 12

SORCERY AND FORTUNE-TELLING

Nineteenth century Gypsy researcher and writer Charles Leland always was at his best when he was describing how he wormed some open secret out of a reluctant Egyptian. Leland traveled far and wide throughout Europe and Asia to debunk superstition and mistaken concepts of Gypsy sorcery and fortunetelling.

People who read about American Indian sorcerers and Gypsy fortunetellers very promptly conclude that they are all phonies or lunatics. They do not realize how these Gypsies, who pass half their lives in wild places watching waving grass and falling waters, and listening to the brook until its cadence speaks in real song, believe in their inspirations. The Gypsies recognize that there is the same mystical feeling and presence in all things that live and move and murmur as well as in themselves. Of the elements, they speak as though they were intimate friends. Of animals, they speak in tones that St. Francis of Assisi might have used when he talked to the animals.

Our technologically-thrust society is the source of an increasingly stressful life style in the 21st Century. The life of television, internet cyberspace, receptions, parties, business offices, factories, stock market, newspapers, cell phones and social networking belie enjoyment of nature. The children in our Western culture are raised in an electronic, plastic world of instant communication.

No one who lives "in the movement" can understand the sweet old sorcery of nature. But nature is eternal and while grass grows and rivers run, man is ever likely to fall again into the eternal enchantments. Until he does, he will have no new poetry, no fresh art, and must go on copying old ideas and having wretchedly worn-out exhibitions in which there is not one original idea. This is more than "going green". It is looking at nature with new eyes.

Know this: the very first efforts of the human mind in the direction of the supernatural were gloomy, strange and wild; they were of witchcraft and sorcery, dead bodies, defilement and deviltry. Men soon began to believe in the repetition of certain rhymes or spells in connection with dead men's bones, hands and other horrors or relics. This old religion exists exactly as it did of yore, whenever men are ignorant, stupid, criminal or corresponding to their prehistoric ancestors. Different people may have different names for their primitive religions, but the premise is the same.

SORCERY AS RELIGION OF PREHISTORIC RACES

The theory in the 19th century, just as applicable in the 21st century, is that spells, fortune-telling and sorcery represent a degraded form of the religion of the prehistoric races, la vecchia religione, as explained by a Florentine soothsayer. Spells are always more efficacious when couched in a tongue not understood by people.

When the Gypsies came to Europe, bringing with them a mass of incantations, mantras, witchcraft and pretensions to occult powers, derived from a religion which was earlier than the Vedas, and which is essentially the same everywhere, they naturally and simply glided into the position of hierophants and priests thereof. Vedas (Sanskrit for "knowledge") are a large body of texts which originated as long ago as 1500 B.C. There are schools of Indian philosophy which cite the Vedas as their scriptural authority. In India, a knavish guru could play upon the fears of the villagers, extorting liquor and port bribes, to "make So-and-so's liver bad", a state of things which one so trusted and reverenced would have plenty of opportunities of accomplishing.

GYPSY REALM OF MAGIC

Magic is the production of that which is not measured by the capacity of the conscious working will. Gypsies are regarded as fortunetelling, witch-doctoring, love-philtering experts on sorcery and magic. But are they? Archeologists and men of science who would have disdained the mere thought of magic are beginning to stray. Hypnotism has revealed great wonders. Memory, the basis of thought according to Plato, which was once held to be a determined quantity, has been proved to be practically infinite and its perfect development to be identical with that of intellect, so that we now see plainly before us the power to perform much which was once regarded as miraculous.

In 1875, Mr. Leland determined that Gypsies have always been the humble priests of what is really the practical religion of all peasants and poor people; that is, their magical ceremonies and medicine. Gypsies have been the colporteurs of what in Italy is called "the old faith" or witchcraft.

Study of the lore of Gypsies shows what happens when the mind of man rejects all sorts of training, intellectual, moral and spiritual and aims, in every direction at that same sort of freedom which the roving Gypsy life attains when it throws off the restraint of fixed abodes.

Gypsies have always lived a life that seeks freedom from society's restraints. Gypsies lead an arbitrary life style, arbitrary in the choice of occupation or idleness and arbitrary in the selection of wild nature which they prefer to civilization, arbitrary in their skepticism and beliefs. English Gypsies have now "gone to brick", they live in houses instead of tent (tan) and caravan (vardo). However, they still maintain the extraordinary weight of superstitions and their own teachings about dispelling misfortunes.

CLOSE OBSERVATION FOR SOOTHSAYING

Soothsaying can be explained away by saying that the Gypsy power is based on very close observation and a very alert memory. These are faculties which we might cultivate to an infinite degree, till they should often become powerful enough to unveil to us the future of those on whose countenance we gaze.

Gypsies, without being able to say why, are often inspired to divine or guess without revealing the process to common sense. They look into the eyes of a person. Something in glances and tones, gestures, mien, and address, suggests at once an assertion or a prediction which proves to be true.

They could be using their dream power. That power has millions of experiences or images at its command. It flits over them like lightening. It can combine, abstract, compare and deduct,

Dream power may make the Gypsy more of a thaumaturgical artist than anything else. The wonder is not that we so often hear of marvelous, magical, inexplicable wonders, but that they are not of daily or hourly occurrence.

The truth is that we have the ability and we are indeed within ourselves magicians, gifted with infinite intellectual power, the ability to know and do many things. Witness the dream spirit that knows all of our memories and which combines, blends, separates, unites, intensifies, or beautifies all persons, scenes, acts, events, tragedies or comedies that we have experienced. The amount of apparitions, dreams, hopes and omens which these latent facilities cause, or seem to cause, is illimitable. No man knows how much he knows. The Gypsy soothsayers tap into and are inspired by this power.

GYPSIES' RELIGION

There isn't any one faith or religion, scarcely even any superstition, which stands forth as the most perfect representation of the opinions of the advanced free-thinker Gypsy . The 19th century scholars who studied Gypsies said that six or seven thousand years of hungry marauding starved God out of the mind of the Gypsy. However, Gypsies everywhere are exceptionally gifted in adapting themselves to the circumstances around them and this applies also to religion. For instance, when the Turks conquered and occupied the Christianized Balkans and favored Islam rather than Christianity, the Gypsy exhibitors of bears, who ambled from village to village with their circus, decided that it would be wise to appear to be either Christian or Mahometan according to the local situation.

The Gypsy idea of God includes the sky and all in it – lightning, fog, wind, rain, air. Earth, to them, is the divine mother of everyone. However, Gypsies are a people who like to have both faith and a faith. They will gladly accept the religion or one of the religions of a country in which they live for some time.

Perhaps the nearest approach to religion which the Gypsies have is their devotion to the dead – a cultus which is shown in very curious ways: a brother or husband will refrain from some usage or indulgence because the deceased wife or sister was addicted to it, or perhaps because the thing had been done or enjoyed for the last time in the company of a beloved one. They also burn all the possessions of the departed, and avoid any future references to him or her, and if a child has been named after him or her, that child receives a new name. Presumably, this reverence for the dead is the only thing which at all indicates that they subscribe to the immortality of the soul.

Gypsies, however, in a most imperfect manner, know something of Christian teaching: they pay reverence to Christ, burning an ash-fire in his honor on Christmas day, because they say He was born and lived like a Gypsy.

Chapter 13

GYPSIES IN LITERATURE AND MUSIC

William Shakespeare's Ophelia in "Hamlet" was a Gypsy. Victor Hugo wrote about the beautiful Gypsy dancer, Esmeralda, who won the hearts of many men, in his 1831 novel, "Hunchback of Notre Dame".

Throughout literary history, Gypsy vardos are beloved by artists and writers of children's books. Jane Austen wrote about Gypsies in "Emma", and Sir Walter Scott, 16th Century courtier and historian, saluted them as stoical in the face of death.

The musical Gypsies of St. Petersburg and Moscow are well known, as well as the Austrian Gypsies who were the musicians in the first Rommany orchestra of that country. The Gypsy music of composers permeates the world of classical music. Flamenco music is Gypsy music. The soul of Spanish Gypsy music lives on in "Carmen" by Prosper

Merimee and adapted by Georges Bizet for the famous opera. Carmen is probably the most famous Gypsy of all. In true Gypsy style, she predicts her own demise: "this bird you are trying to capture will beat its wings and fly away".

THE BAKER'S DAUGHTER

Gypsy researchers from the 19th century determined that there may be as few as 1,400 words that form the whole of the Rommany language, and those words are all connected with physical wants and actions. Handed down from generation to generation for more than 300 years in England, Rommany has not included one single English word in its exclusive vocabulary.

For instance, the story is told that the Gypsy term for an owlet is the "Maromengro's Chavi", or Baker's Daughter. The Gypsy term is based on the legend that declares that Jesus, in a baker's shop, once asked for bread. The mistress was about to give him a large cake, when her daughter declared it was too much, and diminished the gift by one half:

He said nothing,
But by the fire laid down the bread,
When lo, as when a blossom blows,
To a vast loaf the machete rose;
In angry wonder, standing by,
The girl sent forth a wild rude cry,
And, feathering fast into a fowl,
Flew to the woods, a wailing owl.

GIPSY'S WARNING

From the United States, comes the "Gipsy's Warning". This was a song published in Philadelphia, Pennsylvania. By sending 10 three-cent stamps (after all, it was the 1880's) to the publisher, J.H. Johnson, he would send you the music to "Gipsy's Warning":

Trust him not, oh, gentle lady,
Though his voice be low and sweet;
Heed him not who kneels before thee,
Softly pleading at thy feet.

Now thy life is in its morning,
Cloud not this, thy happy lot,
Listen to the Gipsy's warning,
Gentle lady, trust him not.

Lady, once there lived a maiden,
Young and pure, and like thee, fair,

Yet he wooed, he wooed and won her,
Thrilled her gentle heart with care.

Then he heeded not her weeping,
He cared not her life to save
Soon she perished – now she's sleeping
In the cold and silent grave.

Lady, turn not from me so coldly,
For I have only told the truth:
From a stern and withering sorrow,
Lady, I would shield thy youth;

I would shield thee from all danger,
Shield thee from the tempter's snare,
Lady, shun the dark eyed stranger
I have warned thee, now beware!

Take your gold, I do not want it;
Lady, I have prayed for this
For the hour that I might foil him,
And rob him of expected bliss.

Aye, I see thou art filled with wonder
At my looks so fierce and wild
Lady, in the church-yard yonder
Sleeps the Gipsy's only child.

ROMMANY LANGUAGE IS DISAPPEARING

Rommany is a distinct language, understood by very few but the Gypsies of pure blood, guarded by them with jealous care. Gypsies deny its existence and though the original grammar with its inflections and syntax has all but disappeared, the words of Rommany Gypsies in England are the same as those used in Hungary, Turkey and Egypt. The word "Rommany", most likely, is a corruption of the ancient Celtic or Gaelic Romath, pronounced Ro-ma, meaning very good or very good people.

Today the Rommany Gypsies are described as Romani or Roms, and this is the term used by organizations such as the United Nations, the Council of Europe, the British Library, and the United States Library of Congress.

The word Gypsy or Gipsy originates from the Greek word Algyptoi, or the modern Greek gift, in the belief that the Rommany Gypsies originated in Egypt and were exiled as punishment for harboring the infant Jesus. The Biblical account is that, after the birth of Jesus and the warning of the Magi, Mary and

Joseph fled the wrath of Herod by traveling to Egypt.

Researchers in the 19th Century believed that the origin of the language was Indian. Deepest among deep words in India is tat, an element or principle, the essence of being. So it is amusing to have heard Gypsies say that's the Tattoo (tat) of it, meaning thereby the thing itself, the whole of it.

Rommany was akin to Sanscrit, Persian, Arabic, Hindustani, Bengalese and the ancient Gaelic that was spoken in the Highlands of Scotland and in Ireland; and to the Cymric, akin to Gaelic, which is taught and cultivated in Wales. The 19th century professorial contingent determined that the actual language of the English Gypsies is an agglomerate of all these, with a mixture of low English.

The English has both its "slang" and "cant". The French has its "argot"; the German, its "Rothwelsch"; the Spanish, its "Germania"; and the Italian, its"fouresque", all of which have borrowed from this nomadic race the words that are familiar to the vulgar, but that rarely find their way to the lovers of literature and the dictionary. The oldest of the true Gypsy words are exceedingly interesting to the philologist. In the glossaries to the works, which gives occasion to these remarks, are to be found many Gypsy words that were in use before the time of the Pharaohs and long before Greece and Rome succeeded to the heritage of empire and civilization.

The Gypsy will talk about kismet like an Oriental: "A man's kismut is what he's bound to kair – it's the kismut of his see". In English, "a man's destiny is what he is bound to do; it is the fate of his soul (life)". Some men's destiny is better than others. The Gypsy's salutation is the Oriental "Salaam". The words and customs resemble low caste Indian.

Nineteenth century researchers determined that everything pointed to Gypsies being descendants of India, expelled from Hindosan in the 14th century. Why and how are questions not answered.

The singular fact remains that a people speaking the same language were found scattered throughout Europe, and their habits and customs remained unchanged, and they endeavored to keep themselves from the rest of the world. Starting in the 19th century, they were disappearing.

The Rommany Gypsies and their language were doomed to disappear.

Their language was passed down from generation to generation by word of mouth. Their speech is heard only from a scattered few, a poor remnant. In Rommany, there is no word to express mind. There are no such kindly verbs as to hope or to soothe, because these emotions have never been formularized by the Gypsy.

The word used for belief is Wallachian, adopted from the time when the Gypsies obtained goods from the Wallachians on trust, for which they never intended to pay. There is no word for glory. Their very numerals have dropped out, and though the Gypsy can count up to six, and possesses names for 10 and 20, he is put to straits to express seven, eight and nine. He has no names for the months, none for the days, except Sunday, and only a few for the commonest plants, animals and insects. The English Rommany still is more copious than the French and possesses far more of the original Gipsy tongue.

PURE ROMMANY BLOOD

True Gypsies are of unmixed blood, of pure Rommany blood. In Britain, especially, the Rommanys have not always observed their law of marriage very strictly. There have been many marriages between Rommanys and non-Rommanys.

A person born of a marriage in which one partner is a gaujo (non-Gypsy) and the other a Rommany, is by the Rommanies called a posh-rat or "half-blood" (from the Rommany words posh or half and rat or blood). Non-Gypsies would still call that person a Gypsy. If a posh-rat marries a non-Gypsy, their offspring are called didakais: a didakai is a person of less than half Rommany blood.

Genetic studies in the 21st century determine that the Rommany lineage was founded approximately 32 to 40 generations ago, with secondary and tertiary founder events occurring approximately 16-25 generations ago. These estimates emanate from the Rommany language itself which has features of the modern Indo-Aryan languages.

England has tens of thousands of descendants of Gypsies who are not true blood Rommany Gypsies but who celebrate their Gypsy heritage nevertheless. There are few people who know that every time we look from the window into a crowded street, the chances are great that we shall see at least one person who bears in his or her memory Gypsy roots, and that person is English born and English bred.

The Gypsy may be a beggar on the streets, an aerial artist in the circus, a peddler of pottery and baskets at a boot sale or a fiddler at a fair. The Gypsy may be unsuspected by the Gorgios, but they are known to each other and may still speak among themselves, more or less, remnants of Rommany.

It is not the language alone which binds Gypsies together, but a curious inner life and freemasonry of secret intelligence, ties of blood and information, useful to a class who have much in common with one another but very little in common with ordinary citizens.

VICTORIA, QUEEN OF THE GORGIOS

Gypsies tell the story of a happening near Windsor Castle one bitter wintry day, when Victoria was Queen of England from 1837-1901. The snow was lying thick all over Windsor Park when a Gypsy family was crossing it. The tan (tent) had to be suddenly pitched because the mother was overcome with pangs of labor. A few sticks were hurriedly gathered, but there was hardly any time to scrape away the snow and get the fire lit before the Gypsy woman gave birth to twins.

News of the birth of twins in the snow under her window reached the ears of Her Majesty, who at once sent food and drink and clothing to the Gypsy camp. Among the presents were some babies' woolen stockings, which the Queen had knit with her own hands, and a pair of blankets, which but a short time before, it is said, had lain on a state bed.

Gypsies repeat this anecdote with great pride and "the socks knitted by the Queen of the Gorgios" are frequently referred to by them when they speak of deeds of thoughtful and timely charity.

EPILOGUE

EXCERPT FROM DOREEN'S DIARY

Reflections by Doreen as she battles post-polio syndrome: Where were you, God, when the Nazis extermination camps existed and people – Jews, Poles, Czechs, even British POW's little children and babies – were gassed and burned in ovens during the Holocaust in World War II? Where were you, God, or was the devil looking down at the hell that was existing on earth? Why did this happen and why did you not do anything and then I think that could it be that my pain is nothing compared to the above? To understand the future, you must understand the past.

The Second World War – when you have been through dreadful years of world war, you are just happy that your own children and grandchildren were not born in that time. It is so hard for the younger generation to understand the horrors of what went on at that time: the bombs and their terrible destruction of lives and homes.

171

HOLLAND

I had a year of fun traveling by myself before I started my family. I was about 18, a jeweler trainee, and loved my work. My boss sent me by train to his other branch in Holland to be a diamond cutter. I was not wanted at home, so I did not feel that I would be missed. I stayed with a relative of my boss in Amsterdam. I also spent time at the Hague and Schenening. I stayed in Volendam and worked for a jewelry shop there. I loved the Dutch people and learned quite a bit of the Dutch language. I could have stayed in Holland for the rest of my life, but I was worried about my mother. Reluctantly, I came back to the same old dark basement flat where she was living with a new lover. Later, I found a room in Queens Road Gardens and lived there for several months.

LOVE

I am looking forward to leaving this life behind and having no more pain and knowing only peace and love. Love is the most blessed emotion to feel, to never be afraid to show, even though you thought you may not have had enough love in the past. Love is more than words; it is what you do for someone

.

A HAPPY ME

My bedroom is my world. I have everything I want: my TV for entertainment, my books for education, photos of family around me, my Minnie the cat, my windows to glimpse the outside world, my beads for occupation and my bed for comfort and sleep.

JEALOUSY

Jealousy is a very nasty emotion. I have in my life been on the receiving end of jealousy from nasty people. It is due to their own insecurities: talking behind my back, disliking for no reason, other than they want to judge me for any good qualities that I have. Now they talk with me, but I haven't forgotten what they said and did nasty toward me. I will always come out on top. Sad for them.

FORGIVE ME

Forgive me that I know that I am dying, but I have to leave this life and my beloved family. This is beyond my control. It might seem cruel that I ask my family to have my darling Minnie the cat put down because she has been my companion and has known only love and care.

And I quote my favorite poem:

Invictus

Out of the night that covers me
Black as the Pit from pole to pole
I thank whatever gods may be
For my unconquerable soul.

In the fell clutch of circumstances
I have not winced nor cried aloud
Under the bludgeoning of chance
My head is bloody, but unbowed.

Beyond this place of wrath and tears
Looms but the Horror of the shade,
And yet the menace of the years
Finds, and shall find, me unafraid.

It matters not how strait the gate,
How charged with punishments the scroll,
I am the master of my fate:
I am the captain of my soul.
By William Ernest Henley (1849-1900)

BIBLIOGRAPHY

Marie Claire, UK Edition, No. 51, November 1992, "Reading the Signs" by Jane Cameron, page i

The Miami Herald, "Sarkozy: France will not be insulted", September 17, 2010, by Raf Casert, page 9A

Prisoners of War, Gordon Publishing, London, 2000, by Heather Nicholson, Chapter 17, "The Crafty Hag", starting on page 186, cited to Doreen Ingram's experiences as an evacuee child in World War II and was written by Doreen in 1992 exclusively for publication in her Biography

Gypsy Roma Traveler Leeds, permanent site of Gypsy Roma Traveler Communities, Peter Saunders, Manager, http://www.grtleeds.co.uk/home/contact.html

A Few Gypsies, Putnam, London, 1955, by Rupert Croft-Cooke

As Gypsies Wander, Faber & Faber Limited, London, 1953, by Juliette De Bairacli Levy

A Mysterious People, Hamlish Hamilton, London, 1965, by Charles Duff

The Miami Herald, "Report: Czechs Segregating Gypsy Kids", from Miami Herald Wire Services, January 14, 2010, Page 6A

The Miami Herald, "Nearly 100 Gypsies Are Sent to Romania", August 20, 2010, by Julien Proult, Page 20A

Help For The Handicapped, London, by Mrs. Jessica Thomas, 1963, who supervised the evacuation and housing and care of hundreds of children taken from London by bus in 1939; on page 125 she mentions Doreen

The Morning Post, London, "The English Gipsies and Their Language", December 26, 1873

The Standard, London, Letters to the Editor, August 19, 1879

The Gypsies, Houghton, Mifflin & Co., Boston, 1882, by Charles G. Leland, 1882

The English Gypsies and Their Language, Trubner & Co., London, by Charles G. Leland, 1883

The London Spectator, More about Gypsies, November 13, 1882, page 1481

Daily News, London, Gypsy Sorcery, February 17, 1891

The Dialect of the English Gipsies, Asher & Co., London, 1875, by B.C. Smart, M.D., and H.T. Crofton

The Saturday Review, London, "Gipsies", January 16, 1875, page 85

English-Gipsy Songs in Rommany, Trubner & Co., London, 1875, by Charles G. Leland, Professor E.H. Palmer and Janet Tuckey

The Civil Service Review, London, English-Gipsy Songs, July 3, 1875, page 429

The Manchester Guardian, Manchester, short story about a copy of "English Gipsy Ballads" presented to Queen Victoria, July 5, 1875

"Gipsy's Warning", a song, Johnson, Song Publisher, Stationer, Printer and Music Dealer, Philadelphia, PA, 1874

Birmingham Gazette, Birmingham, UK, "Gipsies in the Black Country", January 24, 1874

The Academy, London, Science Column review of "The Dialect of the English Gipsies", Asher & Co., 1875, by B.C. Smart, M.D., and H.T. Crofton, June 19, 1875, Page 637

Gipsy Sorcery and Fortune-TellIng, T. Fisher Unwin, London, 1890, Illustrated by Numerous Incantations, Specimens of Medical Magic, Anecdotes and Tales, by Charles Godfrey Leland, President of the Gipsy-Lore Society, &C.

E.M. Savage Grey is an attorney and former writer and editor with South Florida Newspapers. She is the co-author of "Sex and the Senior Citizen" which was based on 1000 interviews with seniors in Miami-Dade County. Co-author Mrs. Revy Wikler is deceased. The book was the basis of information for a Congressional change in the Social Security law whereby elderly widows could remarry and not lose Social Security benefits.